RENEWA

SAMUEL WEBER

'Weber is probably the only person in his generation who is equally at home in and directly informed about contemporary literary theory and its antecedents in Germany, France, and the US. His theoretical interest in psychoanalysis serves as a viewpoint from which a powerful combination of philosophical, linguistic, and political concerns are brought together in an uncommonly productive dialectical interplay.'

Paul de Man

This book presents the first introductory text examining the work of the contemporary thinker, Samuel Weber. Accessible, compelling and challenging, Weber's writing offers a rewarding investigation into the connections between literary and cultural studies, media and technology, and philosophy and aesthetics, in the context of significant intellectual debates and developments linking Europe and North America. The critical practice of Weber's various texts is explored in detail, along with his studies in philosophy, aesthetics, deconstruction, media, technology, psychoanalysis and theatre.

WITHDRAWN
UTSA Libraries

for Ceri-Ann and Alice May, with much love

Samuel Weber
Acts of Reading

SIMON MORGAN WORTHAM
University of Portsmouth

ASHGATE

© Simon Morgan Wortham 2003

All rights reserved. No part of this publication may be reproduced, stored in a retrieval system, or transmitted in any form or by any means, electronic, mechanical, photocopying, recording or otherwise without the prior permission of the publisher.

The author has asserted his moral right under the Copyright, Designs and Patents Act, 1988, to be identified as the author of this work.

Published by
Ashgate Publishing Limited
Gower House
Croft Road
Aldershot
Hampshire GU11 3HR
England

Ashgate Publishing Company
Suite 420
101 Cherry Street
Burlington, VT 05401-4405
USA

Ashgate website: http://www.ashgate.com

British Library Cataloguing in Publication Data
Wortham, Simon
    Samuel Weber : acts of reading
    1.Weber, Samuel M.
    I.Title
    193

Library of Congress Cataloging-in-Publication Data
Wortham, Simon.
    Samuel Weber : acts of reading / Simon Morgan Wortham.
        p. cm.
    Includes bibliographical references and index.
    ISBN 0-7546-3122-2 (alk. paper)
        1. Criticism. 2. Psychoanalysis and literature. 3. Mass media criticism. 4.
    Weber, Samuel M. I. Title.

PN81.W64 2003
801'.95'092--dc21

                                                            2002190857

ISBN 0 7546 3122 2

Library
University of Texas
at San Antonio

Typeset by Tradespools, Frome, Somerset.
Printed and bound in Great Britain by MPG Books Ltd, Bodmin, Cornwall

Contents

Abbreviations

Works by Samuel Weber

A   'Ambivalence: The Humanities and the Study of Literature', in *Institution and Interpretation*, expanded edn (Stanford, CA: Stanford University Press, 2001), 132–52. (Originally published in *Diacritics*, 15:2 (1985), 11–25, and also included in the original edition of *Institution and Interpretation*, 132–52.)

BS   'The Blindness of the Seeing Eye', in *Institution and Interpretation*, expanded edn (Stanford, CA: Stanford University Press, 2001), 73–84. (Also included in the original edition of *Institution and Interpretation*, 73–84.)

CA   'Caught in the Act of Reading', in *Institution and Interpretation*, expanded edn (Stanford, CA: Stanford University Press, 2001), 180–206. (Originally published in *Glyph*, 1 (New Series) (1986), 181–214.)

CE   'Closure and Exclusion', in *Institution and Interpretation*, expanded edn (Stanford, CA: Stanford University Press, 2001), 3–17. (Originally published as 'Texts/Contexts: Closure and Exclusion', *Diacritics*, 10:2 (1980), 35–46, and also included in the original edition of *Institution and Interpretation*, 3–17.)

CU   'Catching Up with the Past: Discussion with the Weber Reading Group', in *Mass Mediauras: Form, Technics, Media*, ed. A. Cholodenko (Stanford, CA: Stanford University Press, 1996), 168–208.

DC   'The Debt of Criticism: Notes on Stanley Fish's *Is There a Text in This Class?*', in *Institution and Interpretation*, expanded edn (Stanford, CA: Stanford University Press, 2001), 33–39. (Originally published in *Critical Exchange*, 15 (1984), 17–26, and also included in the original edition of *Institution and Interpretation*, 33–39.)

DD   'The Debts of Deconstruction and Other, Related Assumptions', in *Institution and Interpretation*, expanded edn (Stanford, CA: Stanford University Press, 2001), 102–31. (Originally published in J.H. Smith and W. Kerrigan (eds), *Taking Chances: Derrida, Psychoanalysis, and Literature* (Baltimore and London: Johns Hopkins University Press, 1984), 33–65, and also included in the original edition of *Institution and Interpretation*, 102–31.)

FH   'The Future of the Humanities: Experimenting', in *Institution and Interpretation*, expanded edn (Stanford, CA: Stanford University Press, 2001), 236–52.

FU   'The Future of the University: The Cutting Edge', in *Institution and Interpretation*, expanded edn (Stanford, CA: Stanford University Press,

2001), 220–35. (Originally published in T. Smith (ed.), *Ideas of the University* (Sydney: Research Institute for the Humanities and Social Sciences/Power Publications, 1996), 43–75.)

GO 'Goings On: Discussion with Rex Butler', in *Mass Mediauras: Form, Technics, Media*, ed. A. Cholodenko (Stanford, CA: Stanford University Press, 1996), 209–30.

I   'It', *Glyph*, 4 (1978), 1–31.

II   *Institution and Interpretation*, expanded edn (Stanford, CA: Stanford University Press, 2001). (Originally published as *Institution and Interpretation: Theory and History of Literature. Volume 31* (Minneapolis: University of Minnesota Press, 1987).)

LF   *The Legend of Freud*, expanded edn (Stanford, CA: Stanford University Press, 2000). (Originally published in 1982 by the University of Minnesota Press.)

LP   'The Limits of Professionalism', in *Institution and Interpretation*, expanded edn (Stanford, CA: Stanford University Press, 2001), 18–32. (Originally published in *Oxford Literary Review*, 5:1–2 (1982), 59–74, and also included in the original edition of *Institution and Interpretation*, 18–32.)

OO   'Objectivity and its Others', in *Mass Mediauras: Form, Technics, Media*, ed. A. Cholodenko (Stanford, CA: Stanford University Press, 1996), 36–54.

RW   'Reading and Writing—*chez* Derrida', in *Institution and Interpretation*, expanded edn (Stanford, CA: Stanford University Press, 2001), 85–101. (Originally published in *Tijdschrift Voor Filosofie*, 45:1 (1983), 41–62, and also included in the original edition of *Institution and Interpretation*, 85–101.)

TD   'The Divaricator: Remarks on Freud's *Witz*', *Glyph*, 1 (1977), 1–27.

TP   'Taking Place: Toward a Theater of Dislocation', in D.J. Levin (ed.), *Opera Through Other Eyes* (Stanford, CA: Stanford University Press, 1994), 107–46. (Originally published in *Enclitic* 8:1–2 (1984), 124–43.)

TSS 'Television: Set and Screen', in *Mass Mediauras: Form, Technics, Media*, ed. A. Cholodenko (Stanford, CA: Stanford University Press, 1996), 108–28.

UF   'The Unraveling of Form', in *Mass Mediauras: Form, Technics, Media*, ed. A. Cholodenko (Stanford, CA: Stanford University Press, 1996), 9–35.

US   'Upsetting the Setup: Remarks on Heidegger's "Questing after Technics"', in *Mass Mediauras: Form, Technics, Media*, ed. A. Cholodenko (Stanford, CA: Stanford University Press, 1996), 55–75.

Other Works

AH   Derrida, Jacques, 'The Age of Hegel', *Glyph*, 9 (1986), 1–43.

G   Derrida, Jacques, '*Geschlecht* II: Heidegger's Hand', in *Deconstruction and Philosophy: The Texts of Jacques Derrida*, ed. J. Sallis (Chicago, IL and London: University of Chicago Press, 1987), 161–96.

IU   Bahti, Timothy, 'The Injured University', in R. Rand (ed.), *Logomachia: The Conflict of the Faculties* (Lincoln, NB and London: University of Nebraska Press, 1992), 57–76.

LS   Miller, J. Hillis, 'Literary Study in the Transnational University', in J. Hillis Miller and Manuel Asensi, *Black Holes/J. Hillis Miller; Or, Boustrophedonic Reading* (Stanford, CA: Stanford University Press, 1999), 3–183.

O   Derrida, Jacques, 'Otobiographies: The Teaching of Nietzsche and the Politics of the Proper Name', in *The Ear of the Other: Otobiography, Transference, Translation*, ed. C. MacDonald, trans. P. Kamuf and A. Ronell (Lincoln, NB and London: University of Nebraska Press, 1988), 1–38.

OE   Levin, David J. (ed.), *Opera Through Other Eyes* (Stanford, CA: Stanford University Press, 1994).

M   Derrida, Jacques, 'Mochlos; Or, the Conflict of the Faculties', in R. Rand (ed.), *Logomachia: The Conflict of the Faculties* (Lincoln, NB and London: University of Nebraska Press, 1992), 1–34.

PR   Derrida, Jacques, 'The Principle of Reason: The University in the Eyes of its Pupils', *Diacritics* 13:3 (1983), 3–20.

SE   Freud, Sigmund, *Standard Edition of the Complete Psychological Works*, ed. and trans. James Strachey (London: Hogarth Press, 1958).

UR   Readings, Bill, *The University in Ruins* (Cambridge, MA and London: Harvard University Press, 1996).

Preface

Rather than presenting Samuel Weber's 'work' as a wholly intact and continuous body of scholarship or a distinguished instance of critical or philosophical 'development', this study argues that the different and diffuse centres of attention characterizing Weber's writings relate to – or circulate *within* – one another, only to dislocate and continually re-place each other, in a ceaselessly restless yet extraordinarily productive interplay that is as ongoing and unresolvable as it is irreducible. The possible connections that undoubtedly open up between the individual chapters of this book are not, therefore, finally worked to a point of resolution or closure of the kind that often constitutes the ultimate 'object' or ambition of a culminative critical argument aspiring to exhaustive coverage and assimilation of the writings to which it attends. Instead of simply pursuing a comprehensive and uniform line of investigation, then, this book tries, in some way or other, to do justice to such a 'goings on' as is found in Weber's writings.

Beginning with the various questions Weber wishes to raise where certain conceptions of the process or act of reading are concerned, *Samuel Weber: Acts of Reading* also introduces the issue of what is entailed by reading 'in the name of' someone or some *other*. Weber's work shows how reading emerges by way of a complex and ambivalent movement which serves neither to convey and confirm the authority or self-identity of an intention, nor to secure the unity and coherence of the 'object' we are given to read. Reading 'in the name of' someone or some other meanwhile produces complicated effects which not only call into question traditional notions of the 'author' or the 'work', but which uncannily double or repeat their effects so as to continually deform, disorganize, dislocate or displace the forms and concepts which we often assume as implicit, and upon which we frequently rely, when reading the 'work' of another. By attending to these particular questions as they emerge in Weber's writing, this study seeks not only to elucidate Weber's views on such topics, but to *assume* or submit to the effects they entail, so as to *read* Weber 'otherwise', according to a different movement or, indeed, a movement of difference.

The first chapter of the book keeps open the question of reading 'in the name of' an other (or, indeed, a 'host' of others, the very conception of which itself requires further thought), so as to explore the issue of Weber's indebtedness to Derrida, Freud, deconstruction, and psycho-

analysis – among others. Here, such a question of debt remains as
unresolvable as it is inextricable, insofar as Weber's 'work' is concerned.
In the midst of this 'work', we find indebtedness of a kind which appears
virtually impossible to acknowledge adequately, much less to satisfactorily redeem or repay. This 'impossible' indebtedness, however, does
not merely render debt infinite and therefore insolvent, in a way that
might cause (the very notion of) 'debt' to lose its purchase or its force.
Instead, just as it can never sufficiently be recognized, admitted or
dispatched, such debt must nevertheless be *assumed* (for it can never be
entirely *overlooked*). The (unbalanced) assumption of debt happens by
way of a number of ambivalent operations, processes or effects – a
continual 'goings-on' – whereby the irredeemable situation of indebtedness might be considered as somewhat akin to a joke (although whether
serious or flippant, it is virtually impossible to tell).

Chapter 2 attends to Weber's various writings on the question of (the)
institution, in particular to resituate (to dislocate or replace) more recent
debates concerning the 'ruin' of the university in terms of the
significance of a number of texts published over several decades by
both Weber and Derrida on institutional issues. Chapter 3 surveys
Weber's work on technics, technology and media (a series of topics to
which we return in the interview that concludes this book), in order to
raise the question of the specific 'place' occupied by a thinking of
technics and technology amidst Weber's various concerns: aesthetics,
institutions, theatre and so forth. Here, far from transcending the
problem with which it deals so as to provide a secure standpoint from
which to judge the issue, the very question of 'place' in fact presupposes
and concerns 'technics' itself, therefore engaging us in a different and
much more ambivalent movement than might be presumed where one
wishes to treat a 'topic' or 'object' of academic inquiry in the
conventional sense. Technics as a conflicted movement of *emplacement*
(following Heidegger) thus remains extremely difficult to place securely,
leaving us with no safe places – and no secure standpoint – where
technics or technology are concerned.

The problem of how to contextualize or 'frame' specific topics or
issues that interest Weber in terms of the entire body of his work is one
that persists in the fourth chapter on theatricality. Here, Weber's
thinking on the question of theatricality draws powerfully upon the very
problem of the 'frame' for deconstructive thought, whereby, since Kant
at least, the frame can be considered as both an indispensable and an
impossible condition of the 'work'. The delineation, and hence the
demarcation, of an aesthetic object, upon which the very conception of
aesthetic form depends, requires the contour or frame (of the 'work', for
instance) to be, and to remain, clearly distinguishable. Henceforth,
however, the frame itself would appear to have a constitutive function,
serving as 'the enabling limit of the work'. Yet the fact that the 'limit' or

'edge' of the work thus irreducibly partakes of, and participates in, the 'form' which it would otherwise serve to particularize means that, as Weber tells us, 'just this participation would require another frame' for the aesthetic object to be comprehended *as such*. And then, presumably, as this frame once more partakes of its constitutive function as an indispensable element in the composition of form, *another*. And then *another* ... .

The framing (or placing) of a question, problem or issue in Weber's own 'work' – that of theatricality, for example, which itself rests upon a deconstructive thinking of none other than the frame – therefore always takes place *on condition of another*. Thus, the question of debt once more traverses that of technics as *emplacement* or, indeed, that of theatricality as the continual dislocation of aesthetic space or place. The inextricable 'relations' of indebtedness, technics, aesthetics, institution and theatricality – all of which imply uncanny repetitions which hardly secure the self-identity of the Same in the 'work' of Samuel Weber – therefore call for the most scrupulous attention to the question of iterability, raised foremost in (and by) the texts of Jacques Derrida, but assumed with such complex and demanding effects in those of Weber himself. It is here that this study breaks off, takes its leave, via a departure which itself demonstrates how such departing or *leave-taking* is both impossible and necessary. For, if nothing else, iterability entails a certain sort of de-parting or de-part-ure: that is, a divided, redoubling movement which repeats as it separates, returning *as* leaving.

The last word, in a sense, is Weber's – although, of course, his own 'work' powerfully challenges any such idea. The interview that concludes the book sees Weber responding both to a series of questions concerning a range of topics and issues arising from his many texts, and to the dramatic events surrounding 11 September 2001 that unfolded during the short period of time when the interview was conducted. Here, urgent questions concerning media, technology, war, politics and globalization are fielded and developed in a way that not only serves to rearticulate, but which promises to transform, a number of problems having to do with justice, debt, spectatorship, theatricalization, ambivalence, intellectual response and participation itself – problems that help to define Weber's abiding interests and commitments. The discussion which takes place during the final pages of this book therefore serves less to confirm than to extend and redeploy 'otherwise' the thought and work of Samuel Weber.

Acknowledgements

A version of Chapter 2 was originally published as ' "To Come Walking": Reinterpreting the Institution and the Work of Samuel Weber', *Cultural Critique*, 48 (Spring 2001), pp. 164–99.

I would like to thank Samuel Weber for his enormous generosity and patience throughout the writing of this book.

Introduction

Samuel Weber: Acts of Reading

Samuel Weber is an important and influential critic, writer and thinker who has authored many books over several decades, including *Unwrapping Balzac, The Legend of Freud, Institution and Interpretation, Return to Freud* and *Mass Mediauras*. Born in New York, Weber was initially educated in the United States. After graduating from Cornell in 1960, he studied in Europe, mainly Germany, where he encountered the work of the Frankfurt School, and Theodor Adorno in particular. Indeed, Weber became sufficiently acquainted with Adorno to be entrusted with the task of translating *Prisms*, and his translation of, and introduction to, this text helped to define the way in which the ideas of the Frankfurt School would be received in the English-speaking world. Weber himself has since written on the work of Adorno and, to a greater extent, on that of Walter Benjamin. While in Germany, Weber held an assistantship at the University of Berlin under the hermeneuticist and philologist Peter Szondi. He also took part in the Western discovery of the Bakhtin Circle. Weber was co-founder and editor of *Glyph*, a journal which was instrumental in consolidating the reception and reputation in North America of certain varieties of continental philosophy, not least deconstruction, just as an audience for such writing was rapidly expanding during the 1970s and 1980s. If, as David Wills has pointed out, 'It would be easy to rehearse a history of deconstruction in America … a history passing through texts like "Signature Event Context" (1977) and "Limited Inc." (1988)'[1] then Weber has certainly played his part in this history, since both texts were translated by him, and the former was published in *Glyph* alongside one of Weber's earlier essays. He has since occupied a number of prestigious academic positions, serving as program director for the International College of Philosophy in Paris (an institution that Jacques Derrida helped to set up) between 1985 and 1989.

It will already come as no surprise, then, that Weber's work is often closely associated with that of Derrida, and indeed during their careers the two men have crossed paths in an interesting variety of ways. It was Weber, for example, who broke the news to Derrida, by calling him *on the telephone*, of the discovery of certain articles written by Paul de Man during the German occupation of France in the 1940s – a discovery which culminated in the notorious de Man affair, which became something of a landmark in the changing fortunes of deconstruction abroad. (Weber himself wrote a long article on the subject, 'The Monument Disfigured', which was published alongside contributions by a number of eminent scholars in the collection *Responses: Paul de Man's Wartime Journalism*.) Derrida writes of Weber's telephone call, of course, in his essay 'Like the Sound of the Sea Deep within a Shell: Paul de Man's War', and it could be said to take its nevertheless very singular place among a possible chain of telephone calls that crop up in Derrida's texts, among them the 'collect call' from 'Martin', 'Martine' or 'Martini' 'Heidegger' in 'Envois', all of which contribute to a thinking of tele-effects in deconstruction. Indeed, to the extent that Weber's work raises the question of a certain 'indebtedness' to Derrida, and also to de Man, by whom Weber was taught, his telephone call on the subject of de Man's wartime journalism may well operate on the same exchange as the 'collect call' of which Derrida writes in 'Envois', since Weber himself dwells at some length on this 'episode' in his essay, 'The Debts of Deconstruction and Other, Related Assumptions'. The question of indebtedness, that is to say, may be intimately bound up with a thinking of the *call* – the call for, and of, Weber, Derrida, de Man, Heidegger and, of course, the other ('Martine', 'Martini' … ?) De Man, the former teacher, wrote of his erstwhile student that:

> Weber is probably the only person in his generation who is equally at home and directly informed about contemporary literary theory and its antecedents in Germany, France, and the U.S. His theoretical interest in psychoanalysis serves as a viewpoint from which a powerful combination of philosophical, linguistic, and political concerns are brought together in an uncommonly productive dialectical interplay.[2]

Weber is currently Avalon Professor of Humanities at Northwestern University and Director of its Paris Programme in Critical Theory, a programme he previously initiated while Professor of English and Comparative Literature at the University of California. That he has spent many years dividing his time between Europe and the United States perhaps reflects his participation in the encounter between various traditions of European thought and the American critical scene, the intellectual and disciplinary landscape of which Weber has spent a great deal of time describing and explaining while at the same time continuing to read and write about a number of 'European' thinkers and writers (Kant, Kierkegaard, Freud, Lacan, Benjamin, Heidegger, Artaud and Derrida, among others) in a variety of 'European' languages. Yet Weber's books, lectures and essays have made a strong impact elsewhere, such as in Australia, Singapore, and Beijing. Nor is Weber 'just' an 'academic', as his work in German opera testifies. Between 1985 and 1987, for example, he served as dramaturge for the

Frankfurt Opera House, and has worked in a similar capacity in Dusseldorf, Stuttgart and Ludwisburg.

Without taking this short biographical survey any further, it is possible to find reflected here some of the topics and questions on which Weber's work has itself concentrated for several years: disciplinarity, institution and the academic profession; technology, technicity, media and tele-effects; theatricality, scene and scenario; authorship and authority; translation and reading; knowledge and indebtedness; and, indeed, deconstruction's 'wake'. In view of the kind of discussions that take place in Weber's writing, however, the apparent 'repetition' of these themes and issues in the 'life' of the author hardly assume self-evident explanatory force. Nor, given the nature of Weber's work, does such 'repetition' (a motif and movement that assumes much importance, albeit in somewhat different guise, in his texts) allow us to decide upon, determine or resolve the question of the author's intentions in undertaking what one could only hesitate to describe as 'acts of reading'. Rather, the very question or conception of such supposed 'acts' – of authorship, reading and writing – is itself opened up by Weber's 'work': that is, by his 'own' writing and reading. What, then, of the relationship – and one is certainly suggested by the very title of this present study – between 'Samuel Weber', on the one hand, and 'acts of reading', on the other? What, indeed, is significant 'in' or 'about' the punctuative mark that spaces or stages this encounter between the two parts of the title, 'dividing and joining them in a relation yet to be determined' (RW, 92), as Weber himself writes of the *dash* that inhabits (although not quite in a *homey* sense) the title of one of his own essays, 'Reading and Writing—*chez* Derrida'? Let us begin on these questions by reading – and, perhaps, by *dashing* between – two essays by Weber, the relevance of which could not be more obvious than in their very titles: 'Reading and Writing—*chez* Derrida' itself; but, first of all, another text, 'Caught in the Act of Reading'.

Caught in the Act

In this essay, first published in the mid-1980s, Weber examines the work of Wolfgang Iser, notably Iser's major text, *The Act of Reading*. Although his star has since waned considerably, at this time Iser's work was popular and influential. In 'Caught in the Act of Reading', Weber remarks on the peculiarity of this situation. Since Iser's 'theoretical writings' drew on a tradition associated with phenomenology and hermeneutics which lay substantially outside 'the mainstream of North American critical theory' (CA, 180),[3] Weber wanted to suggest that the very 'phenomenon' of his popularity and influence needed some explanation. Moreover, part of this effort to explain the apparent ease with which Iser's work had been incorporated into North American literary criticism and debate also entailed an attempt to distinguish, if only in an implicit fashion, the difference of Iser's work from other 'theoretical writings' drawing on traditions of thought which similarly travelled across continents during the 1970s and 1980s to reach a growing audience in America. Thus, for example, 'Caught in the Act of Reading' has more recently been included in the re-edition of Weber's book *Institution and Interpretation*, where it can now be read alongside 'Reading and Writing—*chez* Derrida', an essay in which deconstruction's 'reading' (in the multiple sense of such a phrase) is, as we shall see, described and enacted in ways that contrast strongly with work of the kind done by Iser.

At the beginning of the essay, Weber cites Stanley Fish's condemnation of Iser's theory. Writing in *Diacritics* in 1980, Fish presents Iser's theoretical project as 'finally nothing more than a loosely constructed network of pasted-together contradictions; push it hard at any point and it immediately falls apart' (cited in CA, 180). Yet Weber shows how even this critical reader of *The Act of Reading* falls prey to its 'seductive charms' (CA, 180). Fish declares that Iser's theory is 'full of gaps [that] the reader is invited to fill ... in his own way' (cited in CA, 181). Yet since Iser imagines the process of reading to involve actualizing the potentiality of the text, which itself remains, from the outset, under the control of what Iser terms the 'blank' and 'negativity', Weber tells us that Fish 'resorts to Iser's own categories in order to dismiss him' (CA, 181). If Iser's 'theory' appears quick to incorporate that from which it might otherwise be set apart, as the example of Fish's rebuttal amply demonstrates, then the effort to distinguish Iser's 'marvelous machine' (CA, 180) – a machine for reading which operates according to notions of 'negativity' or the 'blank' – from others with which it might become confused, specifically fellow travellers across the waters of the Atlantic, becomes all the more complicated a task. That is 'Reading and Writing—*chez* Derrida' is unavoidably at issue once more in 'Caught in the Act ...' – at least, if all is not to be caught up in the act-ion of Iser's 'marvelous machine'.

For Iser, writing at a time of perceived crisis in literary studies, the explanatory power of traditional literary criticism had waned as its hermeneutical activity failed to reduce works of modern art to, as Weber puts it, established 'norms of unity, order, and harmony' (CA, 181). In addition, Iser insists that such criticism was in any case bound to lead up a blind alley or, indeed, a dead-end street. The notion that works of art contained a meaning which could be finally and authoritatively determined was obviously contradicted by continuing literary–critical debate. More to the point, however, the ideal scenario of closure and resolution imagined by such hermeneutical practice would inevitably entail the irrevocable demise of criticism itself, suggesting all its efforts to be unavoidably entropic and thereby self-confounding from the beginning. A criticism whose legitimate function is principally to hasten its own end arguably suffers an obsolescence of a fundamentally originary kind.

Iser therefore suggests that an operational model devoted to studying the process of *producing* effects of meaning in literary works should replace the sacred quest for the *revelation* of meaning that occasions the object of traditional hermeneutics. Since the transformation of the discipline of literary criticism along these lines would seem to require conceptions of the act of reading to be fundamentally revisited and rethought, Iser claims that his theory entails a shift of emphasis towards the reader, insisting that the text comes to life 'in' or by means of the reader. Reading, however, is imagined by Iser to be akin to a process of visualization or image-formation in which meaning is assembled on the basis of 'perspectives' given to the reader as the different elements or parts of the text combine. That these 'perspectives' arise first and foremost from the text, rather than simply from the reading-process itself, implies that there is *another* intention, outside the act of reading, which directs or controls the production of meaning. Put another way, readers do little more than actualize a text which, prior to the act of reading, is already present as potentiality – and, indeed, already present as potential *totality*, inasmuch as it is the text which grants 'perspectives' that allow it to be comprehended in general and *as such* by the reader. But if the text itself determines the process by which meaning is thereby produced, or if it functions to control the operations of reading by which it finds itself actualized as totality, what might be said of this *other intention* that determines the text's controlling force?

Weber writes that, 'Iser's theory stands or falls with its ability to establish the power of the text to control the reader's response, for only then can reading be regarded as a process by which the potentiality of the text is actualized' (CA, 188). If Iser's text seems to exercise a certain degree of control over readings even as antagonistic as that of the theorist Stanley Fish, then what happens when Iser's 'theory' elaborates itself on the basis of 'readings' of its own? In one sense, of course, the very last thing that *The Act of Reading* should be doing is *reading*, since Iser's theoretical endeavour to account for the reading process in general acquires legitimacy only if the sphere of theoretical construction and description transcends the interpretive domain where reading takes place. As Weber puts it, reading 'must constitute the *object* of the theory, not its method' (CA, 185). Iser therefore attempts to depict his engagement with other literary and theoretical texts in *The Act of Reading* as non-interpretive and purely illustrative in relation to his own intentions. He does not read, then, but only draws upon 'authoritative citation' (CA, 186). This leaves us with a very odd situation. By precisely *not* reading the sources to which it amply refers, *The Act of*

Reading cannot be said (on the basis of Iser's own theory) to actualize them at all, so that elaboration or clarification of Iser's theoretical intentions – which place the emphasis principally on actualization itself – can only derive from what is entirely non-actualized in or about these other texts.

Yet Weber is able to demonstrate that Iser's efforts *not* to read precisely entail reading, so that *The Act of Reading* can be shown to participate in, and partake of, that which it must nevertheless exclude and transcend in order to acquire legitimacy as 'a theory of aesthetic response' – the book's very subtitle. Indeed, the theory of reading under construction in Iser's book is actually exemplified – which, as Weber is quick to point out, is not the same as confirmed – in the very process of its elaboration. Thus, for example, in writing *The Act of Reading*, Iser participates in the interpretive activity of 'consistency-building' that he describes as integral to the reading-process. 'Consistency-building' involves both the selection and, inevitably, the exclusion of certain textual elements in order to build comprehension of the text. However, Iser must reconcile such exclusions with his idea that reading actualizes the potentiality of the text as potential *totality*. Finding himself in this dilemma, he cites Ernst Gombrich's apparently authoritative remark, to which Weber draws our attention, that whenever 'consistent reading suggests itself ... illusion takes over' (CA, 186). However, Iser *selects* this description of consistency-building only to *exclude* Gombrich's conclusion that 'illusion takes over'. He argues that the exclusions which occur during consistency-building do not just derive from the illusionistic projections which establish coherence and comprehension on the reader's part. Instead, such exclusions constitute merely a transitional stage or phase in the more extensive process of the actualization of the text from the perspective of totalization that itself constitutes the text's 'intention'. Here, of course, not only does Iser engage in 'consistency-building' on his own part, both selecting and excluding in respect of Gombrich's 'text', but in the process he cannot help but *read* Gombrich. Or so it would appear, at least. For this reading, as unavoidable as it may seem, cannot ever quite get its act entirely together *as* reading. Iser would have us believe that reading, insofar as it entails the effort to build consistency, nevertheless transcends the exclusions of which it must partake in order to occasion the process not just of actualization but of more comprehensive totalization of the text on the basis of the text's 'own' intentionality. Here, then, the projections and illusions of the reader are subsumed within and subordinated to the controlling intentions of the text. That, for Iser, *is* the reading-process. Yet, in going against what Gombrich's text would appear to intend, this is hardly what happens when Iser reads him. On the contrary, if Iser does read him, it is only – on the basis of his own theory – *not* to read Gombrich at all.

Unless, of course, Iser *does* read Gombrich, in the sense that, as Weber puts it, 'in *contradicting* Gombrich's explicit assertions he in fact is *actualizing* their potential *implications*' (CA, 188). This would certainly seem to be consistent with at least one aspect of Iser's own conception of reading, but it would nevertheless entail the effort to build consistency in a way which would seem to resist, rather than submit to, the text's controlling intentions – for Iser, the very purpose or definition of reading. Furthermore, the obviously unstable, non-self-identical image of reading that arises from the entire encounter between Iser and Gombrich here brings us back to the very problem of establishing legitimacy and authority insofar as the 'theory' of *The Act of Reading* is concerned. For what the whole episode demonstrates is that authoritative citation and supposedly detached theoretical description cannot exclude and transcend, but must in fact partake of, and participate in, acts and conceptions of reading which – in their very *différance* and supplementarity – remain difficult, if not impossible, to reconcile or unify in terms of the perspective of totalization. Since such a perspective would, for Iser, of course be an intentional one, the perspective of an intention to be identified with the controlling intentions of the text, the question of authorial control and authority over the reading-process suddenly begins to loom large. Far from presenting us with a theory to be stated or to be cited authoritatively *as meaning just what it is intended to mean*, the danger for Iser is therefore that *The Act of Reading* might, too, be taken by its readers as a text to be *read*, perhaps even in the same way that *The Act of Reading* reads Gombrich while all the while claiming merely to cite this 'authority'. To go further, the danger for Iser may even be that *The Act of Reading* is a text – just like the text of Gombrich that Iser is given to read – which indeed *must* be read if its potential is at all to be actualized in the direction of totalization. As will be evident by now, however, such 'reading' – as never a self-identical activity, never just a straightforward 'act' – would, of course, stymie as much as advance this very same process.

If Iser's theory therefore gets into a great deal of trouble in the very process of seeking to establish, as Weber puts it, 'the power of the text to control the reader's response' (CA, 188), then it is 'negativity' and 'the blank' to which he resorts in the attempt to regain control. Weber explains that, for Iser, the blank:

> ... emerges as the negative embodiment of the potentiality of the text and hence sees to it that the 'wandering viewpoint' does not go too far astray and get lost. It is the blank that prevents the 'segments and cuts' of the text from cutting up uncontrollably by enclosing them within a 'framework.' The blank, in short, by delimiting the 'whole network of possible connections' defines the potential identity of the text and its power to control the illusionary element of the reader's consistency-building. (CA, 188–89)

Negativity, meanwhile, 'is Iser's theoretical attempt to name the "force" capable of controlling the illusionary process of selection and exclusion ... in order for the reading-process to be determined as insight rather than as blindness, as meaning rather than diffusion' (CA, 189). But exactly *how* do these forces acquire and retain control over the process of reading? This is a question which causes Iser some difficulty.

Weber scans *The Act of Reading* once more in order to demonstrate, not for the first time, that the texts resorted to by Iser to provide illustrations in regard to his theory in fact yield implications very different from those Iser would wish them to convey. For example, Iser's description of the novels of Ivy Compton-Burnett implies that, far from being integral to the texts he cites, the 'blanks' that are found here indicate the inability of a specific code, common to all Burnett's characters, to '*impose closure upon the process of selection and exclusion*' (CA, 191) by which consistency is built so as to actualize meaning in the direction of totalization. This common code in Compton-Burnett's novels is a social one, of course, (Weber likens the characters who share it to that other well-known grouping characterized by its own interminable habits and hostilities – literary critics themselves) and it cannot be understood as just an 'internal' property, characteristic or feature of narrowly-defined literary or textual 'form'. For Weber, this raises the question of the *conditions* under which such a code can begin to impose itself, however precariously or impossibly, in the general direction of comprehensibility and closure.

Here, Weber turns to another citation by Iser, this time of Niklas Luhmann's description of systems and systematicity. Luhmann insists upon a principle or conception of the 'system' that the novels of Compton-Burnett indeed demonstrate: since the system is formed by a process of selection and exclusion which is fundamentally non-totalizable, it must be understood as the institutionalization of particularity so as to achieve a degree of stability, however provisional it may be, established on the basis of codes which are shared but specific rather than generalizable. Here, the 'system' bears the hallmarks of an institutional structure in which the forces on which its institutionaliza-tion depend can never be fully incorporated, actualized or totalized within itself. Iser, however, cites Luhmann only to depict the literary system as capable of actualizing *itself* so as to achieve totalization. Institutionalization may well be excluded from Iser's account of the literary system, therefore, but it returns to describe the very process by which Iser's theory is elaborated here. Through the partial and selective 'reading' of Luhmann undertaken by Iser, the latter's own 'system' proves incapable of incorporating fully this 'exteriority' in its own movement towards closure, resolution and totalization. Henceforth, any effects of 'closure' that *are* achieved by Iser's 'theory' or 'system' come at the price of its own non-totalizable particularity, thus indicating a process of institutionalization at work of precisely the kind that Luhmann describes. *The Act of Reading*, then, exemplifies what it is reluctant to acknowledge: that the 'system' posits a degree of coherence and imposes a measure of control on the basis of forces (in regard to the literary system, we recall that Iser names such forces 'negativity' and the 'blank') which acquire their very 'force' only on condition of a process of institutionalization. It is this process alone that can stabilize – if only provisionally – the otherwise interminable play of inclusion and exclusion through which, for example, consistency is built. Yet, at the same time, the system *as* institution can never entirely include the forces at play in its own process of institutionalization. If this is the case, then Iser is not just *wrong* in his contention that the 'blank' and 'negativity' qua 'forces' exercise or exert a controlling intention over the act of reading so as to 'actualize' the text in the direction of totalization: it is in the very effort to elaborate such a 'theory' that this different 'reading' (of the text, of the system, of the reading-process) begins to impose and, indeed, exemplify itself. Moreover, this 'reading' obviously unravels and incapacitates the notion that the 'act' of reading can 'actualize' the text from the perspective of an intention.

Iser's theory of the reading-process assumes, in the definite article of '*the*' reader, an identity *in general* that its very elaboration calls into question. What is shown, instead, is that reading is never just a self-identical act which actualizes a general intention in controlled and controllable ways. As *The Act of Reading* unfolds, then, it is as if reading – or, more to the point, '*the*' reader – finally *cannot* be relied upon by Iser to 'actualize' or 'totalize' the text from the perspective of its intentionality. Going against the grain of a declared shift of emphasis towards the reader, Iser is therefore driven to locate and attribute the intentionality of the literary text in terms of an origin which properly transcends the interminable struggle for interpretive dominance and control among literary critics (as readers) – a struggle that the book itself is designed both to arbitrate and surpass. Since this origin turns out to be none other than the author, Weber tells us that '*The Act of Reading*, which begins precisely by questioning the traditional conception of literature as a repository of univocal meaning, nevertheless gravitates toward the very position it sets out to criticize' (CA, 195). For Weber, such a drift reactivates the entire hierarchical structure that underpins both the 'traditional conception of literature' (CA, 195) – author–text–reader – and the discipline of literary studies – critics–teachers–students – perhaps helping to explain the popularity and influence of Iser's work at a time of perceived crisis in literary studies itself. Despite this drift, however, the space of literature (in which the idea of 'class' acquires a multiple resonance) can never be so securely determined in general or as such, since, as Weber is quick to note, it is an institutional space that is systematized on the basis of its own non-totalizable particularity. Structured, albeit unstably, by the exclusions it seeks to avoid or repress, and able to describe itself only by recourse to particular texts and readings in which it must participate, the conception and discipline of literature in general, like *The Act of Reading* itself, cannot ever quite get its act together.

Reading and Writing—chez Weber

'Caught in the Act of Reading' indicates, then, the limitations inherent in theorizing the process of reading according to conceptions of the literary text as intentional object. Once Iser's text is seen to be caught in the act of an impossible return to traditional hermeutical activity – an act which, *as an act of reading*, can never quite get its act together – the very conception of an *act* of reading becomes as problematical as the idea of the intentionality of the text to which it is inseparably tied. If *The Act of Reading* cannot help but exemplify or *act out* its own theory, and act it out as a process of *reading* rather than just a matter of theoretical description or elaboration, then it also cannot help but act out the impossibility of this theory's transcendence or legitimation – indeed, the impossibility of its 'actualization' or 'totalization' from the point of view of a controlling intention. That is, the theory is *enacted as reading* (and therefore as non-totalizable particularity) which is nevertheless not to be conceptualized as an *act*, if by this is meant the actualizing of an intention.

It should be more than apparent, by now, that Weber's reading of Iser calls into question the very terms of this book's title, *Samuel Weber: Acts of Reading*, unless, of course, one chooses to interpret the title as referring not to the act or acts of reading undertaken by one Samuel Weber, but to Weber's own attempts to analyse the conception of reading as an 'act', and indeed the effects this produces. While this has been an important concern in texts like 'Caught in the Act of Reading', however, one could hardly thematize the entirety of Weber's work in this way. Nevertheless, to take this discussion of *The Act of Reading* as a point of departure in examining the writings of 'Samuel Weber' does alert us, from the outset, to the limitations and dangers of becoming caught in the act of reading Weber's 'works' from the perspective of an intention which might be said to be in control of things, or at home with itself, just as it acts itself out. To conceive of the title of this book as an occasion to juxtapose, in a way that is so deliberately and obviously 'improper', the term 'acts of reading' (which almost becomes a citation here) and the proper name of 'Samuel Weber' is, in a sense, to draw attention to the very impropriety that has been committed, and therefore to demand a very different 'reading' of that which is written or acted out in the work (and in the name) of an author such as Weber.

If it is traditionally the principal purpose and ambition of studies such as these to read 'properly' in the proper name of the author, and thereby to acquire authoritative standing by discerning or closely adhering to the author's intentions, then the necessity of such an 'impropriety' becomes all the more evident if one is to 'read' Samuel Weber differently.

Yet, notwithstanding this 'difference', is it not 'Samuel Weber' (who or what is this?) that nevertheless *must* be read – which I, for one, *must* read – if one is to 'read' the texts to which this study is devoted? Must I not only read 'Samuel Weber' (is this not merely a proper name?) but read also 'his' writing, indeed read and write with him, along with him, alongside him, read and write—*chez* Weber?

If, as we have shown, Weber's writing problematizes the conception and practice of acts of reading, both Weber's 'reading' of others and ours of 'him', then his essay 'Reading and Writing—*chez* Derrida' discusses what it might mean to read and write in the vicinity of the proper name. This vicinity is, of course, never just a 'general' or 'neutral' space – if such a thing could ever be said to be possible. Instead, it gives itself to be thought in terms of particular *place* and *property*, localized and attributed on the basis of belonging *as possession* to that which it designates or accommodates. Property and propriety would therefore appear to demand that the proper name partakes of (an untranslatable) particularity, which pulls in a contrary direction to generalized theoretical construction or description where '*the*' proper name '*as such*' is concerned. Thus, Weber's essay reflects upon the possible meanings and effects of reading and writing in the vicinity of *this* proper name, 'Derrida' – 'Derrida' in particular. 'Derrida', let us recall straightaway, although undeniably a proper name like that of Samuel Weber, is obviously not the same as the proper name, 'Samuel Weber'. In other words, the delimitation of the space of '*the*' proper name, allowing for the theoretical description or elaboration of its general effects, must always be doubled and indeed troubled by the irreducibly particular place which the proper name cannot help but occupy. In this respect, while the writings of the two men share obvious points of similarity, it cannot be assumed that reading and writing—*chez* Derrida would in any sense be just the 'same' (or would establish a footing on the 'same' ground) as reading and writing—*chez* Weber, although of course 'Reading and Writing—*chez* Derrida' is inextricably tied to the proper name (of the author) 'Samuel Weber'. In the midst of this kind of complexity, the question of (im)propriety (of what is proper 'in' or 'to' the name, and what is not), and indeed the issue of the particular place 'occupied' by the proper name, becomes more and more entangled.

In the vicinity of the proper name 'Derrida' it would not seem inappropriate to evoke the distinctive French preposition *chez*, although as Weber goes on to demonstrate it is no more purely 'French' than is

Derrida himself. Rather like the proper name (of Derrida), however, *chez* remains radically untranslatable, at least into the English language in which Weber writes his paper, while at the same time continuing to be thoroughly caught up in a complicated network of cultural translation and transfer traversing the borders of Europe and beyond. As Weber acknowledges, the topic of his paper presents problems not just because of 'the obvious and massive difficulty of defining a subject as enormous as it is elusive, since it can be equated with every aspect of Derrida's work' (RW, 87) – that is, reading and writing 'in' or 'with' or 'concerning' Derrida. Instead, rather like the title of the present study, the very heading of Weber's essay, hanging as it does on this untranslatable (yet always translat*ed* or translat*ing*) *chez*, presents difficulties which are themselves 'intimately bound up with the topic I am about to address' (RW, 87).

To translate *chez* simply as 'in' or 'within' ('in the work of … ') is misleading since, as Weber discovers, *chez* derives from the Latin, *casa*, which, despite our expectations to the contrary, is 'not inscribed in the lexical chain that goes back to the Greek *domos*' (RW, 90) or its intimate relation, *oikos*. *Chez* does not just abide in the 'homely' or 'homey', nestling cosily so as to express the values and meanings one associates with domesticity and interiority. *Casa* signifies instead 'a hut, cottage, or shepherd's cabin' (RW, 90), an outpost or outhouse which is located away from the centre of the homestead or estate, just as the etymology of *chez* situates it 'on the periphery of what might be called the domestic economy of the House' (RW, 90). To translate *chez* as 'in' or 'within' is deceptive enough, therefore; but, in any case, as Weber notes, it is 'especially misleading in regard to a thinker, one of whose major motifs has always been the reassessment of the values of interiority, immanence, and inherence' (RW, 87) and, indeed, who has always paid rigorous attention to the inside/outside opposition which structures their meanings and effects. Moreover, such a translation ('in the work of … ') would indicate the possibility of straightforward attribution in terms of the identity of the proper name and person of the author as intentional agent, which becomes especially inappropriate in regard both to the concerns and the very *manner* of Derrida's writings.

If an adequate translation of *chez* will not 'come' to Weber, having himself begun to wonder of this title proposed to him by the host of his lecture, 'whether it could ever really be "my" title at all' (RW, 89), the author of 'Reading and Writing—*chez* Derrida' decides instead to 'go' – or *dash* – towards *chez*, via a lexical–etymological survey of its antecedents. *Casanier*, for instance, meaning 'homebody', finds its origin in *casenier*, which in turn is derived from *casana*, in Italian 'a bank'. *Casenier*, then, refers to an Italian merchant residing in France. 'Like its referent, the word itself is an émigré' (RW, 90), notes Weber. Through the migrant displacements of language and translation, the émigré is found to abide, at root, in the stay-at-home. *Chez* remains on (condition of) the move. *Casemate*, meanwhile, 'another Italian émigré, this time from the word *casa-matta*' (RW, 90) means, literally, a madhouse. Figuratively, it designates a phoney or false house, and may be associated with *matar*, which, in Spanish, means 'to kill'. The madhouse may not be too far away from the slaughterhouse. *Case*, originally meaning small house or cottage, later refers to a square or box, the spatial dimensions of which may be reproduced on a game-board. Today, however, *case* indicates the highly structured cellular subdivision and compartmentalization of space, as would be found in pigeonholes, while the meaning of *caser* relates to the safekeeping of belongings. Yet 'this most organized member of the family *chez* also bears the marks of the disorder it seeks to master: the *casier* is the inscribed record of infractions' (RW, 91). Not surprisingly, then, *casa* gives rise to *casino*, 'a house of organized, authorized transgression, and above all, games of chance' (RW, 91).

Genealogical investigation of the family roots of *chez* reveals Weber's 'unprepossessing preposition' (RW, 91) to be abundantly hospitable to a motley assortment of intruders and interlopers, serving less to flout 'the economy and laws of the household' (RW, 91) than to *invite* reinterpretation of them. Which is to say that the improper may be, quite improperly, entirely proper to the proper law and economy of the house and, by extension, to the place and property of the proper name. *Chez* opens up the grounds of the property and propriety it denotes to an errant movement (a *dash*) which persistently disrupts the unicity of the proper name as that which secures an abiding identity between the 'work' and the person or intention of the author ('in the work of … '). Notwithstanding the irreducible particularity of proper names, hence-forth reading and writing—*chez* Derrida and reading and writing—*chez* Weber may be no more properly distinct than they are reducible to the 'same'.

Bearing all this in mind, then, how might one read or write, not just 'with', 'alongside', or 'in' ('in the name of … '), but *chez* … (*chez* Derrida, *chez* Weber …)? Insofar as *chez* retains a continually fraught, utterly fragile yet nevertheless constitutive relation to (the language of) interiority, *chez* would appear to be 'in' deconstruction. Deconstruction, of course, does not designate a general procedure or strategy with which both Weber and Derrida are associated so much as indicate a principle, a process or an effect already at work within Western thought, specifically within the metaphysics of self-presentation. If, in the texts of Jacques Derrida, it is writing that acquires prominence at the limits of closure of this metaphysics, then we have already seen how conceptions and practices of *reading* – when construed in terms of notions of intentionality, totalization, actualization, and so forth – re-engage this metaphysics of presence 'in' deconstruction. Nonetheless, Weber is quick to remark a certain 'dissymmetry' between writing and reading in Derridean deconstruction:

> If writing is the ambivalent locus of the most intense investment of Western thought in its effort to systematize itself, and hence the predestined object of any strategy bent on revealing the limits of that system, the place and status of reading appears to be far more modest, less interested and less interesting. The disseminating description of writing as the repressed but irrepressible Other of Phonocentrism would seem to hold, *a fortiori*, as it were, for reading as well. Reading could thus be determined as the effort to reduce difference and repetition to a minimum, the effort of a representation to efface itself before that which it represents, in this case, the text, but without impinging upon or usurping the originality of its model. This interpretation of reading, however, would add nothing new to the general scenario of supplementarity or *différance*: the effort of reading to reduce its repetitive–representative nonidentity with the text would be condemned from the start: if it succeeds, it fails, betraying the text by excess of fidelity, as it were, usurping the latter's prerogatives, taking its place or presenting itself as the double of writing; but if it fails, this too would condemn it to the very difference it seeks to efface; reading would fall short of its goal, its telos, the re-presentation of the text itself.
>
> Considered in this light, then, reading adds nothing new to the drama of deconstruction; it merely repeats it: if writing is presented, within the closure of metaphysics, as the representation of a representation, as the signifier of a signifier, the repetition of a repetition, then reading appears only to reiterate all that once again, adding hardly a wrinkle. (RW, 92–93)

Rather like the traditional kind of literary criticism perceived to be in crisis by Wolfgang Iser, reading seems to be damned if it does and damned if it doesn't. Thus, it would appear that reading is bound merely to repeat or replay the ambivalent and constitutive doubling of writing in regard to 'speech' or 'the metaphysics of presence' (although, of course, the very problematics or dynamics of such 'doubling' hardly leave much room for talk of 'mere' repetition here). In addition, if in contrast to speech, writing is customarily derided as evincing a 'fall into alienated exteriority' (RW, 93), Derridean deconstruction would be keen to distinguish itself from any attempt, such as is made by a critic like Iser, to call upon reading 'to function dialectically, as the negation of a negation' (RW, 93) in order to actualize or animate the 'dead letter' (recalling once more that 'Caught in the Act of Reading' cannot help but reinscribe itself in the project of 'Reading and Writing—*chez* Derrida'). However, to characterize Derridean deconstruction in these ways is tantamount to acknowledging that, to borrow a phrase from Weber, 'reading *as such* would seem to have no independent role to play' (RW, 93) – which, in a certain respect at least, would seem to draw Derrida *closer* to Iser, rather than simply allowing the former to be distinguished from the latter. (Here, once again, the play of the proper and the improper suggests itself.) Hence, Weber is himself keen to find more *interest* in this idea that reading has no 'proper' place in deconstruction, especially if, as he asserts, the latter is 'directed precisely *at* the *Proper*' (RW, 93), suggesting perhaps that the improper, with all its exappropriative force, is what is proper to deconstruction. If it is to be accorded no proper place in the drama of deconstruction, within which writing acquires prominence at the limits of closure of the metaphysics of presence or self-presentation, reading may well entail a repetition of that (in)to which it appears to be drawn – writing.

However, Weber draws attention to the transformative, altering power and, indeed, the disruptive force of such repetition which is precisely not a 'proper' one; a repetition which is, undecidably, both properly improper and improperly proper in regard to that which it repeats. Reading undoubtedly 'folds itself in with the rest', but it 'cannot and does not leave repetition or its effects unaltered, simply the same' (RW, 96). Borrowing, however improperly, from Derrida's *La Carte postale*, reading can henceforth be assigned a more interesting or decisive 'place' – or, rather, *movement* – by Weber, as part of 'a structure of alteration without opposition' (RW, 97) – one of (improper) circulation that never (properly) comes full circle. Consequently, reading can be envisaged less as the *telos* than the *tele* of writing. If, as Derrida teaches us, the missive can only arrive on condition of the possibility of non-arrival, so that, in a sense, non-arrival is the condition of the postal effect, then reading repeats such an effect only to proscribe what is then generally inscribed – 'return to sender'. As the *tele* rather than the *telos* of writing, reading doubles and replaces writing in a movement whereby the latter can never come home or be found at home, *chez soi*. The 'proper' turns out to be uprooted by the improper which inhabits and repeats it.

To read and write—*chez* Weber? This seems an invitation to make ourselves at home, to put ourselves in his place. But read the postcard again. It is we, who are reading, – who are to be dispatched. We are, along with the host, to be turned out of doors. We must dash.

Notes

1 See David Wills, 'Jaded in America', in Anselm Haverkamp (ed.), *Deconstruction is/ in America: A New Sense of the Political* (New York and London: New York University Press, 1995), 250–62 at 250. Also included in this volume is Weber's essay, 'Upping the Ante: Deconstruction as Parodic Practice', 60–75.

2 Cited in Alan Cholodenko's postface to Samuel Weber's *Mass Mediauras: Form, Technics, Media*, ed. A. Cholodenko (Stanford, CA: Stanford University Press, 1996), 232.

3 Due to the widespread availability of the expanded edition of *Institution and Interpretation*, in contrast to that of *Glyph*, 1 (New Series), in which 'Caught in the Act of Reading' originally appeared, all subsequent references to this essay in the body of my text are to the version reproduced in the former title.

Chapter 1

Debts: To and of Psychoanalysis (Among Others)

Assuming Debt

Perhaps we should go back and start again (which, as it turns out, may also be to begin once more where we left off). For it could be said that Samuel Weber made his name by writing on psychoanalysis rather than deconstruction. Early texts published in *MLN* and *Glyph* in the 1970s, although by no means devoid of reference to Derrida's work, were to devote attention to various aspects of Freud's writing in particular. Subsequently, it was his two books on psychoanalysis which brought Weber critical acclaim. *Return to Freud: Jacques Lacan's Dislocation of Psychoanalysis* was originally written and published in German in 1978, while *The Legend of Freud* first appeared in 1982. Indeed, his next book, *Institution and Interpretation*, which explores issues of interpretive conflict and their relationship to processes of institutionalization, includes complex and influential writings that draw extensively on readings of psychoanalytic texts. Here, essays such as 'Reading and Writing—*chez* Derrida' and 'The Debts of Deconstruction and Other, Related Assumptions' offer critical readings of deconstruction by way of a return to Freud and, indeed, an exploration of Derrida's engagement with him, most notably in *The Post Card*. Of the different texts included in *La Carte postale*, it is perhaps 'Spéculer – sur "Freud"' which is of the most interest, since here Derrida retraces the strategy or scenario of 'making a name' for oneself: in the case of psychoanalysis, a 'pseudonymic' name which Freud makes for himself, one which confuses species and genre. In various ways, across the body of his writing, Weber shows the importance that the *name* of Freud holds for both psychoanalysis and deconstruction – indicating perhaps the irony that Weber's *name* has itself been made by virtue of writings which frequently dwell on the operations, implications and effects of this *other* name, Freud. How this 'debt' is to be assumed or repaid, just how it is 'owed' and whether indeed it is 'owned', poses itself as a question which remains closely tied, of course, to the kinds of reading of psychoanalytic texts, and indeed of 'deconstructive' ones, undertaken by Weber.

Since it would be difficult, to say the least, to dispense with them easily, any reader of Weber or Derrida will have occasion to return to these texts on the name and indebtedness of Freud and of psychoanalysis. In brief terms, however, they allow Weber, via Derrida, to ponder the notion that, 'in contrast to more traditional sciences and disciplines, psychoanalysis is bound up with the name of its founder' since 'its specificity is indissolubly linked to a fundamental indebtedness' ('Borrowing is the law', as Derrida puts it – the law of psychoanalysis, in the multiple sense of such a phrase), so that 'something like a proper name is required to hold it together' (DD, 108). 'But for this very reason', writes Weber, 'the "property" of that name will be even more fragile than is ordinarily the case in regard to the sciences' (DD, 108). Indeed, Weber suggests an affinity between, on the one hand, the necessarily fragile reduction of the entire discursive practice of psychoanalysis to the proper name of 'Freud' and, on the other, the 'noncontingent limitation at work in the Oedipus complex' described by Derrida in *La Carte postale*, whereby the latter – the Oedipus complex – constitutes itself as a 'reductive, regulative fiction, a part masquerading as the whole' of what Derrida describes as the 'nebulous matrix' of the *fort-da* (DD, 106–107). As Derrida points out, what goes under the name of 'Oedipus' might be said to distinguish only one of the 'threads' or 'sons' of this 'nebulous matrix, with its chains of fusions or fissions, its permutations and commutations without end, its disseminations without return' (cited in DD, 106).[1] Nevertheless, as Weber notes, it becomes extremely difficult to account for such apparently unavoidable or 'noncontingent' reduction, when just such reduction would seem to be 'the condition of the possibility of *accounting* in general' (DD, 107). This aporetical situation surrounds the oedipal reduction being discussed here, but also presumably envelops the circumstances in which the complexly and unstably interwoven matrices of 'psychoanalysis' are reduced to the name of 'Freud'. From this point onwards, then, the 'noncontingency' under discussion means that one cannot dispense with an account of, as Weber puts it, 'the manner in which an irresistible process of repetition assumes the aspect and the allure of a *proper name*' (DD, 108). Yet such repetition is one of the *fort-da* discerned, as we have just seen, in psychoanalysis, which more specifically plays itself out in a process of doubling which ties the conditions of *possibility* of the account to the conditions of *impossibility* of accounting itself (since an account can happen only on condition of the very same reduction which the account is itself required to describe or explain). If the proper name acquires its 'allure' only via a process of reduction which ties it to a repetition that must be accounted for *as a function of the reduction that gives us the proper name*, and yet for which one can never adequately account, then the fragility of the proper name in regard to the 'nebulous matrix' which provides its setting suggests not just impossible possibilities, but imposes relations of desire, debt, disavowal, possessiveness and guilt in this 'interminable story', as Derrida has put it, of the making of a name.

Derrida's argument is that Freud anticipates the fragility of the proper name in regard to this 'nebulous matrix' with its 'disseminations without return', and he seeks to overcome it by attempting or pretending to prepay what Derrida terms 'the charges of a return-to-the-sender' (cited in DD, 108).[2] Such a strategy nevertheless engages a disparate variety of techniques. Sometimes Freud is driven to assert his independence of mind, and thereby to confirm the self-authorizing legitimacy of his psychoanalysis, by denying or dismissing its indebtedness – to Nietzsche, for example – while, on other occasions, the debts of psychoanalysis would seem to be acknowledged so readily and entirely, assumed so radically and absolutely, that they appear quite irredeemable, quite unrepayable. For Derrida, the debt is thus rendered 'either infinite or insolvent' (cited in DD, 109)[3] so that the very notion of 'debt' henceforth tends to lose its force. The distinctiveness of Weber's essay, however, consists in his attempt to dispute this idea that a debt thus generalized to an infinite degree ('Borrowing is the law ...') comes to be more or less invalidated and effectively inoperative. For the discussion of reduction and repetition in respect of the 'nebulous matrix' and the proper name suggests that, once the notion of debt begins to lose its force, so too would the dynamic and unstable energies that impel and, indeed, compel the (impossible) process of accounting, including an account such as the one given in 'Spéculer – sur "Freud"' by Derrida himself. Debt, for Weber, is not so easily dispatched. Rather, he turns to Nietzsche's discussion of *Schuld* – debt and guilt – in *The Genealogy of Morals*.

Nietzsche is able to uncover an historical shift from the notion of *Schuld* as redeemable debt to that of *Schuld* as unredeemable guilt. This, in turn, allows for Nietzsche's hypothesis on the origin of 'the guilty conscience'. The 'guilty conscience' is tied to the resentment which develops out of a noble or aristocratic culture, in the process undermining the opposition between nobility and *ressentiment* which more generally structures Nietzsche's text. The transition from an 'older', more 'material' notion of *Schuld* as repayable debt to that of *Schuld* as irredeemable guilt occurs when an unproblematic standard of measurement or equivalence is lost. But how is it lost? 'It is striking to note', says Weber, 'that this loss, the key component of the genealogy Nietzsche is developing, coincides with the emergence, precisely, of something like a genealogical consciousness' (DD, 116). This gives us occasion, perhaps, to recall once more the aporetical condition of *accounting* in general, as that which inevitably involves a certain *repetition* – doubling itself, here, in the 'genealogy of resentment' as the explanation of *loss*: from such relations unavoidably arise those of debt, loss and guilt, as we have already seen. Such devastating 'loss', giving rise to the 'guilty conscience', then, is to be associated with the emergence of a 'consciousness' which itself partakes of, and impels, that which it describes: 'the genealogy of resentment'. The origin of this consciousness, however, is identified by Nietzsche with the self-interpretation of the identity of the community, which takes shape on the basis of an acknowledgement of a debt owed to the ancestors of the present generation. As the community develops and prospers, so the debt grows to disproportionate proportions: it becomes *immeasurable*. Far from discharging the duty owed to the forefathers, the accomplishments of the community place it ever deeper in debt, so that, as Nietzsche tells us, 'in the end the ancestor must necessarily be transfigured into a *god*' (cited in DD, 117)[4] – the origin of the self-identity of the community henceforth being located *elsewhere* – a *god* who is to be *feared* as much as revered. That the transition from *Schuld* to *Schuld* – from repayable debt to irredeemable guilt – is so smoothly narrativized here may serve to mask Nietzsche's complicity with the interpretive violence of a 'genealogical consciousness' which itself coincides with the emergence of resentment. In this light, *The Genealogy of Morals* can be seen to partake of that which it describes, therefore becoming an example of the 'phenomenon' whose origin, rather like that of the indebted and guilt-ridden community itself, is situated *elsewhere*. This calls us to rethink the terms in which we might approach Nietzsche's account of the origin of the 'guilty conscience', of course.

For Weber, nonetheless, Nietzsche's interweaving of guilt and debt 'should sensitize us to the possibilities of dealing with *Schuld* other than those of affirmation or resignation' (DD, 120) – *pace* Derrida. For Nietzsche's account of the spiralling generalization of unredeemable debt, and the manner in which his genealogy partakes of the structure and effects of debt-guilt that it describes, certainly does not entail, as Weber puts it, the 'neutralization or nullification' (DD, 120) of debt – on the contrary, in fact! *The Genealogy of Morals* calls us to witness the interplay between guilt and debt playing itself out via 'the irreducible reference to a certain alterity' (DD, 120): for instance, to the manmade gods of resentment's 'guilty conscience'; or indeed, via another scene of origination, to the deities called forth in the 'prehistorical' world so as to witness the spectacle of suffering by which 'compensation' is conspicuously extracted from the indebted other; or even to the 'genealogy of resentment' to which Nietzsche's 'guilty conscience' may be indebted. In all these examples, the subject of debt – both 'oneself' and an 'other', thus acquiring the uncanny aspect of a revenant that never fully returns – must continue to participate in (although never quite 'own') a guilt-debt which persists and proliferates *in the very play of the affirmation and cancellation of debts*. The returning force of alterities that never quite come home mean that debts can neither simply be settled nor easily dispatched, but may be assumed via a movement which 'retrace[s] one's dislocation by forces that one can neither determine nor identify; to "assume," in this sense, is both to admit an irreducible dependency, and also to refuse that dependency as a mere "assumption": to recognize the "other" at the very moment one tries to take hold of it' (DD, 126). Since one cannot merely 'assume' debt so as to smoothly assimilate or incorporate the 'other' *on which one depends*, debt – even, and perhaps especially, *assumed* debt – is always going to be, in a certain sense, the debt of another. Such 'irreducible reference to a certain alterity' which structures the relations of *Schuld* therefore means that the process of assumption can never just entail 'taking on', but is inevitably also one of 'taking off', to borrow terms Weber has used on a number of occasions. In this sense, Weber's speculations on debt begin to translate themselves into the postal code, recasting debt as part of 'a structure of alteration without opposition': one of a certain circulation that never quite comes full circle – *tele* rather than *telos*. For even if the letter is returned to the sender, this does not resolve the question of debt: who pays the return postage, if not generally the postal system itself, which therefore tends never quite to 'make ends meet'? Weber's debts, Derrida's debts, Freud's debts, Nietzsche's debts, other debts, debts of the other: perhaps these may be assumed, although never quite 'owned' in the multiple sense of such a term, when they are translated into the postal code, where debts never entirely devolve upon either the sender or the addressee, but remain part of a (non-totalizable) system whose accounts are ongoing, never quite achieving balance or closure.

Freud's Psychoanalysis: Conflict and Debt

What, then, of those indebted to Freud, or to Freud's psychoanalysis?

Such a question arises from the very beginning of Weber's *The Legend of Freud*. Here, Weber establishes his point of departure by tracing the history of the founding of the International Psychoanalytic Association (IPA) in 1910, the defection of Alfred Adler just one year later, and, within a further two years, the break with Jung, upon whom Freud had intended to 'transfer' his authority. As the official association of those connected with Freud's psychoanalytic movement, the IPA was established, Weber tells us, primarily to act as a 'supreme tribunal' (*LF*, 36) committed less to challenging misrepresentations of psycho-analysis from *without*, than to distinguishing psychoanalysis proper from what tended to be seen as rogue contenders or impostors *within* the field of psychological investigation. Weber therefore implies that the background to the establishment of the IPA might be explained less in terms of the hostility encountered by psychoanalysis at the turn of the twentieth century, than by the extent of its popularization during the pre-war years. But how is it possible to account for the splits and conflicts that so rapidly came to characterize the early years of the IPA, as the very institution that was specifically intended to maintain and promote the unity, identity and integrity of the psychoanalytic movement itself? The efforts made by Ernest Jones to explain away the frictions and increasing disunity among the psychoanalytic community as simply, in Weber's terms, 'a kind of infantile malady ... destined to disappear with increasing maturity' (*LF*, 36) begin to founder alongside Jones's own admission that, in contrast with the other scientific disciplines, the results of psychoanalytic investigation were in fact particularly susceptible to subjective interpretation. Here, perhaps unwittingly, Jones's insight opens up the possibility of a perspective which both surpasses and incorporates the question of the individual competencies or deficiencies of practitioners of a relatively new 'science', so as to suggest that *in structural terms* the very institution of psychoanalysis itself gives rise to the possibility of conflict and disarray.

Attending to the question of the loss of Jung in 1913, Weber centres on the term Freud himself used to describe his intention to assign authority to his protege: 'transference'. However, with the defection of Jung, such transference happens 'negatively', with a concomitant reversal of roles normally expected in the analytic situation qua therapy. Now, it is the transferring subject – Freud himself – who acts in a conscious and voluntary way, while the 'object' of the transfer – that is, Jung – remains hamstrung by unconscious drives or motives. Or so Freud would have us believe. Here, as Weber tells us, the 'force of the unconscious, by implication, manifests itself ... not in the act of transferring, but in the refusal to accept what is being transferred' (*LF*, 37). Yet, of course, such a 'refusal' in a situation explicitly described as one of 'transference' cannot help but call into question the supposedly authoritative procedures and processes of psychoanalysis itself, especially when the transferring subject here is Freud himself, and the subject of transference is nothing less than his authority. Faced with this obvious challenge not just to his supremacy but to the legitimacy of the claims of Freudian psychoanalysis, Freud nonetheless states an explicit preference for avoiding polemical denunciation of his erstwhile disciples, although, as Weber goes on to demonstrate, while Freud aspires merely to distinguishing and demarcating psychoanalysis proper in relation to variant psychological theories, he unavoidably succumbs to the temptation to devalue other, competing ideas and practices. But, nevertheless, Freud's reasons for wanting to defend psychoanalysis in a more disinterested and dispassionate way could hardly be clearer. As Weber puts it, psychoanalysis, 'although a theory of conflict, is according to Freud itself a most unsuitable medium of conflict' (*LF*, 38). Polemical exchanges, of the kind Freud ostensibly wishes to avoid, inevitably tend to confound the clear-cut roles of the analyst as 'superior' and the analysand as 'subordinate', as dictated by the analytical situation. As Freud himself observes, if the analyst yields to polemical interpretation, then the validity of his analytical insights risks being subsumed under the force of polemical counterinterpretation on the part of the analyst and, up to the point where it is no longer possible for an impartial third party to determine the truth of the matter. Such a scenario would, of course, severely jeopardize the authority (of psychoanalysis) that is here in the process of being defended. Yet if, as Weber tells us, Freud's psychoanalysis cannot help but be drawn into the very confrontation which, for perfectly good reasons, it wishes to avoid, then the question is: why?

Returning to Freud's project of distinguishing psychoanalysis proper from other psychological hypotheses and explanations, Weber detects – in the very effort to describe how the theories of Adler and Jung depart from the essential foundations of psychoanalytic doctrine – a more fundamental distinction at work in the Freudian text, having to do with 'the very mode of thinking that produces theoretical insight' (*LF*, 40). Thus, Freud discounts the Adlerian 'system' as (in contrast to psychoanalysis) *too* systematic, seeking to incorporate and explain an array of 'objects' and phenomena within a general and unified 'theory' which, according to Freud, scarcely wishes to acknowledge the extent of its limits. For Freud, Adler's theory therefore functions along the lines of 'secondary revision', of the kind to which the dream-work subjects dream-material. 'Secondary revision' names the operation by which, in Weber's terms, 'a semblance of rationality, a specious intelligibility' (*LF*, 42) is discerned in the 'material' of the dream. Far from allowing disclosure or explication of the original or ultimate meaning of the dream itself, then, secondary revision works to conceal the *dissimulation* of the dream, 'reorganizing and presenting its material in a manner that seems to conform to the logical and rational expectations of the waking mind' (*LF*, 42), as Weber puts it, so as to render the dream 'acceptable', while at the same time throwing the dreamer entirely off the scent. Hence, so far as Freud is concerned, the 'result is that precisely those dreams that seem most coherent and transparent are in reality the most deceptive' (*LF*, 42).

Reading across a variety of Freud's texts, Weber finds that psycho-analysis tells the story of the historical appearance of systematic thinking, first of all in terms of the rise of animism. Animism, for Freud, entails the effort to reduce the universe to a single unity, to be apprehended from the sole viewpoint of animism itself. However, as Weber tells us, the 'animistic attempt to comprehend the external world in terms of unity and totality corresponds to the newly formed unity within the psyche: the narcissistic ego' (*LF*, 42). By organizing and interpreting the world in terms of a unifying intelligibility such as is demanded by the emergence of the ego, systematic thought reveals itself to be narcissistic as much in origin as in design. And if Adler's theory is *too* systematic, and thus an exemplary case of 'secondary revision', for

Freud it thereby suggests itself as a prime example of the narcissistic ego reacting to defend its inevitably fragile and specious cohesion against the centripetal energies or dislocating dynamics of the conflictual force-field from which it emerges: that of the unconscious. It almost goes without saying, of course, that this sounds like the most ingenious way imaginable to entirely discredit a competing psychological theory – henceforth, Adlerianism can be deemed to be not merely ignorant of that about which it speaks, but actually complicit in the kinds of deception that keep us all in the dark!

However, such an explanation or interpretation of the Adlerian 'system' and its deficiencies hardly leaves Freudian psychoanalysis in a comfortable position, for a number of reasons. At the most obvious level, the theoretical aspects of psychoanalytic hypothesis or explanation henceforth become as problematic to defend, or indeed *assume*, as they are impossible to eschew or discount. Moreover, the unavoidably systematic quality of psychoanalytic investigation can hardly be divorced from the unifying or integrative intelligence of 'a point of view' (and, in *The Interpretation of Dreams*, Freud himself does not baulk at acknowledging this very same connection, although of course he is much less reflective in uncritically adopting the *standpoint* of the male ego in his description of the castration complex) – a 'point of view' which psychoanalysis itself considers a dissimulation of the kind undertaken by 'secondary revision' in regard to the dissimulations of the unconscious. On the other hand, if it is Adler or the Adlerian 'system' that Freud associates with 'secondary revision', in contrast to Freudian psychoanalysis, which founds itself on the unconscious, then it is not just the case that the *defector* conceals his dependency on that which comes to be associated with the authority of Freudianism. For even if psychoanalysis proper were to be allied more closely with the unconscious than with the processes of 'secondary revision' (which must nevertheless be considered indispensable to its rational and scientific disposition) then the unconscious, it must be recalled, is responsible for dissimulating its operations in the dissimulation practised by secondary revision. As Weber notes, this would imply that, 'as with the unconscious, the interests of psychoanalysis, as an institution, would depend on a certain kind of self-dissimulation, just as the dream, to fulfil its function, must dissimulate *both* its true nature, and also *that* it so dissimulates' (*LF*, 47). To align Freudianism with the unconscious would therefore seem to provide no more solid a foundation from which to discount the Adlerian 'system', or, for that matter, any competing theoretical knowledge or analytical practice. Indeed, to follow this path would result, however paradoxical it may seem, in a similar situation to the one we might expect if psychoanalysis simply proposed itself as somehow a 'better' system than that of Adler. For in either case, psychoanalysis risks acknowledging its basis in deception, concealment and duplicity. And either way (even at the point of any such self-recognition), psychoanalysis cannot help involving itself in a *self-deception*, whether it seeks to comprehend and master the unconscious through rational and systematic thought or investigation or whether it pretends to forego such rationality in the interests of a closer affinity with the unconscious, which, in *The Interpretation of Dreams*, Freud himself construes less as an origin or latent content than a 'particular *form* of thinking' (cited in *LF*, 102)[5] which always and everywhere dissimulates its intractably deformative character by creating a representational façade, a semblance of intelligibility.

The conflictual force-field of the unconscious, wherein unstoppable processes of deformation or decomposition are continually dissimulated, giving rise to the fulfilment of wishes that nevertheless remain hopelessly conflict-ridden and self-deceiving just where things seem to become lucid, can therefore also be taken to characterize the institution of psychoanalysis, regarding not only its structural propensity towards conflict, division and disarray, but relating also to those effects of duplicity, blindness and ambivalence that attend the polemical crossfire by which its identity and authority come to be posited, defended and challenged. And, of course, this returns us to the question of debt. For in the vicinity of this conflictual force-field that so characterizes the institution of psychoanalysis, *Schuld* (guilt-debt) remains and redoubles itself *in the very play of the affirmation and cancellation of debts*, playing itself out amid a heterogeneous series of effects: transference, defection, authority, polemic and (underlying all these, perhaps) the wish-fulfilment of the narcissistic ego and its nevertheless ineluctable dependency on an alterity which can never satisfactorily be reduced to the image of an outsider. (Elsewhere in *The Legend of Freud*, Weber therefore succinctly observes that: 'psychoanalytic theory sets itself apart in an ambivalent movement that both disperses itself in categories that overlap and converge with each other, and at the same time projects its constitutive dislocation as an outward movement of heretical divergences, as a "falling away" (*Abfallsbewegung*) it can then appear to confront and condemn' (*LF*, 61).) Here, then, the subject of debt in regard to Freud's psychoanalysis (both 'oneself' and the 'other') acquires, once again, the uncanny aspect of a revenant which, like the unconscious itself, never quite succeeds in returning (to itself). The force of alterities that *remain* yet never quite come home (and the 'unconscious' may be only one among a possible host of names we could assign here) mean that the debts of 'psychoanalysis', the debts to or of 'Freud', can neither easily be settled nor simply renounced. Psychoanalysis, in a certain sense, is more or less nothing other than *Schuld*. To assess Weber's debts to Freud, entailing a reading of his work on Freudian texts, involves us in – *obliges us to draw upon* – a line of thinking about psychoanalytic theory and writing, in which the question of such indebtedness only registers itself in an account of the debts of psychoanalysis – an account which, as we've just seen, could never be closed or balanced. In other words, Weber's debts to psychoanalysis can hardly be accounted for without acknowledging an intractable obligation to account for the debts *to*, *for* or *of* psychoanalysis 'itself' – debts which, since they can never be entirely 'owned' (possessed or repossessed, held or withheld, admitted, submitted or acknowledged, construed as 'property' or a 'property' of ...) can hardly hope to be settled (settled up, settled upon ...). Once more, then, such debts devolve neither simply upon the sender or the addressee, but remain part of a (non-totalizable) 'system' – a postal code – whose accounts are always ongoing. And since, if we want to assess Weber's debts to psychoanalysis, we are obliged to draw upon or to credit the line (a line of credit?) Weber takes in relation to the question of psychoanalysis's debts (for on what account could there be foreclosure here?), our 'indebtedness' must become an inextricable part of the accounting that is going on.

All this means that such indebtedness cannot be overlooked, although, of course, neither can it be overlooked in the 'other' sense that it cannot ever be definitively grasped, located, comprehended, mastered, acknowledged or accounted for from a single or transcendent 'point of view'. In the vicinity of debates about the debts of or to psychoanalysis, that much is clear. So the (structural) necessity and impossibility of overlooking our indebtedness here only repeats and renews, rather than resolves, the (entire question of) debt.

Indebtedness: To and of the Joke

As everyone knows, the joke is pretty much over the moment someone tries to explain it to you. If, as Freud contends, the essential characteristic of a joke remains inseparable from the burst of laughter it occasions, then what is distinctive about it simply cannot be done justice, cannot adequately be accounted for, in the aftermath or absence of the laugh (which itself radically interrupts the capacity of explanation so far as the conscious, rational subject or individual is concerned). Yet, if a joke is genuinely a joke, its true measure is that we cannot help but laugh – although, in that uncontrollable instant, we cannot ever truly know exactly what it is we are laughing at. In structural terms, therefore, the joke bears some of the hallmarks we've associated with debt or indebtedness. When it happens, our laughter implies that the joke can no more be affirmed than it can be denied. It simply cannot be *overlooked*, in the double sense of this term. If the joke is, necessarily, over in an instant, the necessarily impossible prospect of *overlooking* it means that it must nevertheless somehow *remain* or persist: the joke is in fact far from exhausted when the laughter dies away. Yet this 'persistence' of the joke cannot be construed along the lines of the kind of repetition that would permit recognition of the joke's self-identity. For, far from impelling a renewed explosion of laughter, the repetition – in a conventional sense – of the joke would cause it to implode. If it is never quite exhausted by the laughter it occasions, and without which, Freud tells us, it simply cannot *be*, the joke somehow *goes on*, precisely at the expense of closure, balance, accounting and recounting (in other words, at the expense of its own self-identity). That is, the joke, if it is a joke (which, of course, it can never simply *be*), depends irredeemably on a situation of incalculable *debt*. Such a situation of debt (the debts of, to or for psychoanalysis, for instance) may, likewise, be considered a joke.

But at whose expense *is* the joke? And who does it leave in debt? Freud? Weber? Another, us, anyone? If we've already suggested that debts such as those of psychoanalysis can never be 'owned', but that the subject of debt is always both 'oneself' and an 'other', let us recall nonetheless that Weber disputes the idea he finds in Derrida that the radical generalization of debt tends to neutralize or nullify indebtedness so far as *anyone* is concerned. Notwithstanding the finally unaccountable movement or spiralling circulation of indebtedness (somewhat akin to the amplifying volume of spasmodic pulsions of laughter, to which one is forced to attend although which one can never really 'understand'), the debt, like the joke, must always be 'on' someone. Although upon whom exactly the joke (or, indeed, the debt) actually *is* – since it never quite *is* – may not ever be entirely clear.

Weber's writings on Freudian texts pay a great deal of attention to Freud's treatment of the problems associated with laughter and joking, so that the issue of Weber's indebtedness to Freud can no more overlook the question of the joke in or for psychoanalysis, than that of debt itself. (Of course, the joke doesn't just crop up 'in' psychoanalysis or, indeed, 'in' Weber's writings 'on' Freud. Jokes are always 'on', in the sense that they are 'at the expense of …'). Essays on laughing and joking in *The Legend of Freud* can be related to a wider body of work on the topic, including articles such as 'The Divaricator: Remarks on Freud's *Witz*', published in the very first edition of *Glyph* in 1977, and 'Laughing in the Meanwhile', appearing in *MLN* in 1987. In 'The Divaricator', Weber examines Freud's theory of the *Witz* so as to ask: 'does meaning constitute *an* or even *the* essential dimension of the joke?' (TD, 15). Initially, Freud wants to insist that what is fundamental to the joke concerns its form rather than its content, not least since jokes reactivate 'the childish pleasure of pure play' (TD, 15), as Weber puts it, seeking liberation from the restraints of the order and logic of 'meaning'. Meaning, indeed, only comes into play as a ruse of the joke, distracting or assuaging the forces of reason so as to eliminate the obstructions posed by reason's inhibitionary character. Elsewhere, in 'Jokes and their Relation to the Unconscious', however, Freud draws a distinction between the jest and the full-blown joke in terms of the 'substance and value' (cited in TD, 16)[6] – the meaning – which may be accorded the latter. In the context of this apparent tension underlying the Freudian conception or determination of the joke, Weber turns to the phenomenon of nonsense jokes. The nonsense joke, argues Freud, is less hostile than merely indifferent to the laws and logic of meaning. However, in a footnote to this particular discussion, Freud asserts both that the joke draws its force simply from a frolicsome style of play that is nonchalantly indifferent to meaning, and that it continues to be motivated by the ruse or lure of a semblance of intelligibility, which deliberately panders to reason's demands in order more radically to subvert or suspend its inhibitions. At this point, Freud turns to the kinds of joke-like productions that seem to present us with mere 'silliness in the guise of wit' (cited in TD, 18).[7] Such quasi-jokes, to which Freud assigns the name *Aufsitzer*, serve, he tells us, to 'rouse the expectation of a joke, so that one tries to find a concealed sense behind the nonsense. But one finds none: they really are nonsense' (cited in TD, 18).[8] Nevertheless, as Weber points out, such jokes cannot be entirely nonsensical, due to the very fact that they can be attributed a purpose: to dupe the audience, not merely to convey the joke but to *play* one upon the listener. Furthermore, for Freud, this purpose may even be related to that of an intention on the part of the teller of the joke, who achieves a certain degree of pleasure in 'taking in' his audience, irritating the hearer by purposefully leading him up a blind alley. The teller of the nonsense joke, therefore, would seem to have no 'object' other than, as Weber puts it, 'the calculated deception of another subject, who has only the possibility of recouping his losses by himself repeating the tale' (TD, 19). This obviously has consequences for a psychoanalytic theory of jokes, especially since the *Aufsitzer*, in seeming to combine an ultimate indifference to meaning with the aggressive deception of reason, cannot merely be relegated to the sidelines of Freudian theory, but instead might be considered the best, rather than the worst, of all possible jokes. For if the nonsense joke is, in a sense, 'the' joke *par excellence*, nevertheless psychoanalysis simply couldn't help but be 'taken in' if it were to take the *Aufsitzer* as a privileged or exemplary 'object' (in the classical sense) of theoretical knowledge and rational description. The *Aufsitzer* would have the last laugh at the expense of psychoanalysis, which itself could only hope to recoup its losses by repeating the tale in a way that ensured its audience was similarly 'taken in'. Yet, of course, the costs of such a strategy would be as incalculable for psychoanalysis as they would remain unavoidable. Here, as Weber tells us, the 'most conspicuous effect would be to reinscribe the subject of theory, and of interpretation, in the charged context of an operation of story-telling, which splits the unified subject of theory into the duplicity of the narrator and the delusion of the listener: each, in some sense, a mirror-image of the other and each engaged in a most ambivalent game' (TD, 19).

If the operations and effects of the *Aufsitzer* are strongly reminiscent of the processes of secondary revision which characterize the self-deluding aspects of all systematic thought or theoretical discourse, then the relation of the *Aufsitzer* to psychoanalysis carries implications and importance going far beyond the particular concerns of Freud's theory of the joke. The *Aufsitzer*, impossible to relegate to merely a supplementary consideration or specific region of psychoanalytic investigation, once more involves psychoanalysis in incalculable expenditure or expense, interminable recouping, irredeemable debt, beyond all possible recounting, accounting, balance or closure. Yet, as should be obvious by now, the question of indebtedness in regard to the *Aufsitzer* cannot be confined to the concerns of psychoanalysis alone. Debts of the kind incurred by the *Aufsitzer* cannot so easily be accounted for.

In *The Legend of Freud*, Weber suggests that the closest translation in English for the *Aufsitzer* is 'shaggy-dog story', and he ends a long chapter devoted to this very topic by retelling what appears to be just such a 'story', one which, he informs us, 'I heard many years ago and at which, if I remember correctly, I once laughed' (*LF*, 156). However inconclusive it may be to finish with such an anecdote or joke – especially, as we shall see, given the 'substance' of the tale – the *Aufsitzer*, as we know, invites reasoned explanation or the attribution of conclusive meaning only to have a last laugh on the listener or interpreter, reinscribing theoretical description, determination or for-mulation as merely story-telling, and leaving the recipient or subject of the *Aufsitzer* little choice but to recount the tale amid (or, indeed, *as*) incalculable relations of expense and expenditure, recouping and debt. Perhaps it is no wonder, then, that Weber's chapter 'ends' in this way. In this context, the 'substance' of the 'story' with which Weber 'concludes' is as pertinent as the timing of its delivery:

A Jew and a Pole are sitting opposite one another in a train. After some hesitation, the Pole addresses the Jew: 'Itzig, I've always been a great admirer of your people, and especially of your talents in business. Tell me, honestly, is there some trick behind it all, something I could learn?' The Jew, after a moment's surprise, replies: 'Brother, you may well have something there. But you know, you don't get anything for nothing – it'll cost you.' 'How much?' asks the Pole. 'Five zlotys,' answers the Jew. The Pole nods eagerly, reaches for his wallet and pays the Jew. The latter puts the money away and begins to speak: 'You will need a large whitefish, caught by yourself if possible; you must clean it, pickle it, put it in a jar, and then bury it at full moon in the ground where your ancestors lie. Three full moons must pass before you return to the spot and dig it out ....' 'And then?' replies the Pole, puzzled: 'is that all?' 'Not quite,' smiles the Jew in response. 'There are still a few things to be done.' And, after a moment's pause: 'But it will cost you.' The Pole pays, the Jew speaks, and so it goes on from Cracow to Lemberg. The Pole grows increasingly impatient, and finally, having paid all his money to the Jew, he explodes: 'You dirty Yid! Do you think I don't know your game?! You take me for a fool, and my money to boot – *that's* your precious secret!' And the Jew, smiling benignly: 'But Brother, what do you want? Don't you see – it's working already!' (*LF*, 156)

Since Weber merely narrates rather than interprets this shaggy-dog story, I will forego any close analysis or thoroughgoing interpretation of my own, which in any case would inevitably fall foul of the snares and ruses of the *Aufsitzer* as much as it might hope to shed light upon the meaning or 'substance' of the tale – if there is indeed any 'substance' or meaning, independent of the form the joke itself takes. For the story undoubtedly involves and recounts incalculable relations of expense, indebtedness, and recouping of the kind we might associate with the *Aufsitzer* itself: the duplicitous *recounting* of the Jew leaves the Pole both completely out of pocket, and yet utterly indebted for the lesson which tells him how to 'recoup' – and perhaps better – his losses at the *expense* of another (although also, by implication, to the ultimate *benefit* of this other). The 'meaning' or 'substance' of the story may therefore be nothing other than that of the *Aufsitzer* itself; and yet what the story shows us, if anything, is that the *Aufsitzer* proceeds (and profits) only by way of a series of red herrings (conveying a semblance of meaning, substance or intelligibility) designed to throw the listener off the scent. If we are tempted to suggest that the meaning of the story is somehow an 'economical' one, then not only are its precise economics far from simple to account for, but they constitute the proceeds of the *Aufsitzer* itself, which no-one can easily calculate or recount.[9]

No less pertinent, however, is the question of just who recounted this story, first heard by Weber 'many years ago'. It was, we are told in a footnote, none other than Jacques Derrida. At least, if Weber remembers correctly – for, by his own admission, he cannot be sure of the circumstances surrounding the joke, told him so very long ago, including whether or not he laughed. (To recall laughter is also, in a sense, to acknowledge its irredeemable loss amid the transitoriness that characterizes at least one aspect of joking, so that such recollection must necessarily also entail a certain lapse of memory or forgetting albeit of that which was never truly 'known' or 'understood' on the occasion of laughter.) And how do we know Weber is even *trying* to tell the truth about this tale? He prefaces its delivery by acknowledging (or, at least, by *feigning* to acknowledge) 'my frustration at so much uncertainty'

(*LF*, 156) surrounding the joke and the *Aufsitzer*, and he resolves to 'mute' this very same frustration precisely by retelling the tale. If he were indeed being serious or artless here, this assertion would place Weber firmly in the position of one upon whom the *Aufsitzer* has had the last laugh, and who can only vent his irritation by recounting the shaggy-dog story in a way that allows the loss to be recouped (or bettered) at the expense of another. Indeed, the entire import of his discussison of the *Aufsitzer* seems to allow for no other conclusion. And yet, if Weber is, indeed, now cast in the role of the story-teller of the *Aufsitzer*, just how easy would it be to separate and distinguish his genuine purpose or intent from the ruse or lure that characterizes the *Aufsitzer* itself? Is Weber serious or is he only joking when he implies that, due to his frustration with the subject-matter at hand, he'd prefer the last laugh of the *Aufsitzer* to be on us rather than him (albeit a last laugh from which, like the Pole, we might ultimately benefit)? To convey as much, in a spirit of utmost honesty or sincerity, would hardly be the best preparation for a 'good' joke, which as we know depends on the lures and traps associated with the *Aufsitzer*. Indeed, since we know that the *Aufsitzer* involves a situation in which the duped listener soon turns duplicitous story-teller, we may wonder whether the joke has already started before it has begun – right here, in the midst of apparently genuine acknowledgement or sincere revelation of the *Aufsitzer*'s 'frustrations'. In the most obvious sense, Weber is joking *during* the recounting of this little shaggy-dog story but, as the recipient or subject of the *Aufsitzer*, isn't he also, in a necessary or structural sense, joking *beforehand*? In this respect, Weber's retelling of 'Derrida's' shaggy-dog story as obviously a joke may, unless we are careful, throw us off the scent of another joke being played here. Of course, where the *Aufsitzer* is concerned, we can never really know for sure. But the undeniable *possibility* of this opening of the borders of the joke or of joking certainly casts doubt upon Weber's apparently ingenuous claim (which comes afterwards, in a footnote) that the joke was told him by Derrida. This causes us to wonder what sort of acknowledgement of debt would it be (unless one were joking), to name or identify Derrida as the – necessarily duplicitous – joke-teller, and perhaps even to imply that Weber's indebtedness to Derrida might somehow be bound up with the latter's aptitude for joking as a species or instrument of duplicity? Clearly, one might be prompted to take this 'moment' in Weber's writing less as a naïve reinscription of the grounds and terms by which Derrida has been criticized, condemned or dismissed (laughed at?) over 'many years', than as a playful and irreverent response to more simplistic versions of the master–disciple relation, according to which the connection of these two thinkers might otherwise be understood. Yet even here, in asserting this explanation or interpretation, we should beware of the ruses and lures that constitute the *Aufsitzer* as a perhaps

more elaborate joke – one that is played precisely at the expense of
intelligibility's self-delusions. That is, one cannot take for granted the
possibility of determining the indebtedness of Weber to Derrida
according to the motif of the *Aufsitzer*, since the intelligibility of this
motif may itself be a ruse of the *Aufsitzer*. For this very 'reason', the
notion impresses itself upon us once more that Weber may be joking
(whether or not, indeed, he *means to*) when he declares Derrida to be the
one who told him the joke.

Yet if the *Aufsitzer* is nonetheless at play here (and we could never be
sure, once and for all, since the *Aufsitzer* can no more be determined as
a clear-cut 'object' of recognition than the relations of the 'sensical' and
the 'nonsensical' which ostensibly constitute its specific form can ever be
convincingly demarcated or stabilized) then this play has, as perhaps its
most telling consequence, the effect of reinscribing 'the subject of
theory, and of interpretation, in the charged context of an operation of
story-telling, which splits the unified subject of theory into the duplicity
of the narrator and the delusion of the listener: each, in some sense, a
mirror-image of the other and each engaged in a most ambivalent game'
(TD, 19). Such a game would be all the more tellingly ambivalent since
it does not function to posit two clearly differentiated participants
engaged in a tactical struggle, however complex this may be: the
duplicitous narrator on the one hand (Derrida, perhaps, or Weber) and
the deluded listener turned story-teller on the other (Weber, perhaps, or
even ourselves). More fundamentally, it 'splits the unified subject' in a
'highly charged context' of story-telling's manifold operations, in which
duping and duplicity, fooling and being fooled, can never quite be
articulated or defined as distinct and separate qualities, properties or
intentions, but remain intractably entangled in and by one another. We
can never finally *tell* who is being duped and who is being deceitful,
since (to return to the language and problematic of debt) any such
recounting or accounting is itself always incalculably split. Amid the
effort of such tale-telling, 'one' may well dupe 'another' but also
(inseparably) deceive, delude and divide 'oneself'.[10]

Notes

1   Here, as elsewhere in this book, I refer to those texts treated by Weber by citing his
    quotations rather than by making reference to the original source in the main body
    of my text. For consistency, this is because Weber frequently presents his own
    translations of texts not originally written in English, or at least occasionally
    modifies the translation. In this instance, Weber refers to Jacques Derrida, *La
    Carte postale* (Paris: Flammarion, 1980), 362.
2   The reference here is to *La Carte postale*, 353.
3   See ibid., 415.

4 Weber quotes from Nietzsche's *On the Genealogy of Morals* (New York: Random House, 1967), 88–89. However, he does note that the translation by W. Kaufmann and R.J. Hollingdale is 'occasionally modified'.

5 See SE, 5, 506–507.

6 See SE, 8, 121.

7 Ibid., 139.

8 Ibid., 128.

9 The 'economics' and 'economy' of the joke receive a great deal of attention in *The Legend of Freud* and in Weber's earlier articles on laughter, joking and psychoanalysis. Much more could be said on this topic, via careful and detailed reading of Weber's own analyses here. In particular, however, Weber explores and questions Freud's assertion that it is a 'principle of economy' which unifies the different facets of the *Witz*, constituting its fundamental character. According to Freud, the pleasure derived from relieving psychical expenditure, not least in respect of the lifting of inhibitions and thus of the energy-expenditure required to maintain them, aligns the *Witz* with a certain tendency to compress or save. However, the economy suggested by one kind of reduction would appear to be more than balanced by the expenditure of intellectual effort entailed by the joke technique itself. Freud's own – unanswered – question, of who then saves and who gains, once more raises the matter of unbalanceable accounts and unreedemed debts (as well as that of the conflictual force-field constituting the subject of the joke). In the sections of *The Legend of Freud* devoted to the psychoanalytic treatment of jokes, Weber also explores the inevitable shortcomings, in the Freudian text, of an 'economic' description of laughter; and in 'Laughing in the Meanwhile' we find a preliminary attempt to relate laughter to a thinking of the gift. Finally, in regard to this issue of the 'economy' or 'exchange' of the joke, it is also worth noting the following remark by Weber in the section of *The Legend of Freud* called 'The Shaggy Dog': 'The contract that binds the parties engaged in the joke ... diverges from that of liberal, bourgeois jurisprudence: the contracting parties agree to a process of exchange without being certain that they will be able to accomplish the obligations they incur' (*LF*, 149). This quote is perhaps especially significant when considering the last part of the present chapter, regarding Weber's recounting of a joke apparently told him by Jacques Derrida. The 'parties engaged in the joke' here might be the Pole and the Jew, Derrida and Weber – among others.

10 Might it be possible that the Pole in fact *doubly* dupes the Jew, artfully dispossessing him of his secret so as to extract a surplus or profit in terms of the benefit ultimately derived from the proceeds of the *Aufsitzer*, while at the same time merely feigning annoyance or irritation so as to pander to the Jew's narcissistic self-assurance that, ultimately, he remains in control of the *Aufsitzer*? In this case, a semblance or ruse of meaning, purpose, rationality (the Jew's apparent 'masterful-ness') might be being promoted and exploited (via the Pole) only in order to lift, more fundamentally, the obstructions or inhibitions standing in the way of the *Aufsitzer*'s proceeds or its play. Yet even if the Jew is deluded or divided against himself, the very same goings-on will doubtless apply, in turn, to the Pole ... of whom no-one (not even himself) can ever be sure if he 'fools' or is 'fooled' by the Jew.

Chapter 2

Reinterpreting the Institution

During the early to mid-1980s Jacques Derrida wrote and spoke extensively and explicitly about questions relating to institutional issues, not least as a response to his strong involvement in GREPH[1] and the setting up of the International College of Philosophy. During the same period, Samuel Weber wrote a series of essays on various aspects of the question of the institution, all of which appeared individually as chapters and articles, before being collected together in a single volume, *Institution and Interpretation*. This was first published in 1987 and has been highly influential for subsequent projects – such as, for example, Peggy Kamuf's *The Division of Literature, Or, The University in Deconstruction*. However, partly due to the agenda-setting impact of Bill Readings' analysis of the commercialized university of excellence in *The University in Ruins* (an analysis which imposed itself, no doubt for good reason, upon the collective consciousness of significant sections of the academic community), Weber's work on the academic institution seemed generally to have been a little overlooked during the 1990s, at least in more explicit debates about the future of universities today. Perhaps to address this situation, *Institution and Interpretation* has now been reissued with additional material, much of it written in the wake of Readings' work. Indeed, the lasting value of *Institution and Interpretation* is suggested by the addition of this new material, which in fact renders possible fresh insights into Weber's earlier work on the question of the institution, while simultaneously offering new ways to take forward debates concerning *The University in Ruins*, beyond the current tendency either simply to accept and reinforce the terms of Readings' account, or to underplay, if not disregard them, altogether. In his more recent writing on the university, Weber offers a respectful yet penetrating critique of Readings' thesis, which in turn requires a careful rereading of Weber's own contribution to the thinking of the institution over the last 20 or so years.

In this chapter, I want to demonstrate how such a rereading of Weber might take shape: both to suggest the relevance to contemporary debates about the university of just about all his writings on the topic; and to highlight the way in which particular combinations and *re*combinations of various, recursive elements and concerns character-izing Weber's writings reveal significant possibilities for reactivating important elements in a broader tradition of deconstructive thinking on the question of the institution – not least in the work of Jacques Derrida himself. (Here, more generally, it is not so much a matter of attending to the specificity of Weber's critical contribution by distinguishing where possible between different conceptual renderings, frameworks, or emphases that would carve out a precisely articulated relation to Derridean thought, as it is a question of appreciating the *iterative* relation of Weber's work to deconstruction, as well as to psychoanalysis and other theoretical or critical projects, whereby, in much less clearly differentiated ways – in terms of hard conceptual distinctions at least – repetition offers itself for Weber as a performative mode of transformation in each singular case, according to the specificity of the analysis or object of study.) If taken alone, without due consideration to a context of reading established by his own work (as well as the work of others, like Derrida), Weber's responses to recent critics, such as Bill Readings, can seem somewhat enigmatic. When restored to such a context, however, they become extraordinarily fruitful and pertinent – indeed, they begin to seem like the tip of an iceberg.

The Movement of Knowledge: From Adequation to Ambivalence

Weber introduces *Institution and Interpretation* with a discussion of Gaston Bachelard's 1930s text, *The New Scientific Spirit*. This he takes as indicative of a larger awareness within a number of academic disciplines that a decisive shift has taken place during the twentieth century in the formation and orientation of scientific – and, by extension, humanistic – knowledge. For Bachelard, the operations and discoveries of the new approach, foremost in the fields of mathematics, physics and chemistry, render problematic the traditional standing of an 'adequation' conception of truth in which human thought is separated from the object of inquiry such that the priority of the latter is asserted over the former. (We might note that such a long-standing conception of 'adequation' may well have seemed to invert the hierarchies underpinning the traditional divisions of Cartesianism, but nevertheless profoundly reinforced its terms. This is important, as Weber's work on the institution is threaded through with a series of reflections on Cartesianism, as we will see.) Rather, with the emergence of a new spirit of scientific endeavour, 'cognitive objects are henceforth to be identified not by reference to an intrinsic quality, their *form*, but rather by their capacity to be *deformed* and *transformed*' (*II*, xi) as the process of cognition unfolds. Discoveries relating to, for example, the impossibility of 'establishing simultaneously the position and velocity of an electron' or demonstrations of the fact that 'the instrument of measure, the photon, alters the object in the very process of measurement, and similarly has its own frequency modified in the encounter', radically undermine 'the traditional conception that holds space and time to be fixable and measurable in terms of "the point and the instant"' (*II*, xi). In short, the customarily referential language and discourse of science – one that imagines itself to be basically extrinsic to the 'objective' phenomena with which it is concerned – has, in the last 100 years, encountered new-found complexities, inhabiting both the natural world and the various contexts and conditions of modern scientific experimentation, that it can simply neither contain nor survive.

One of the implications of this new scientific spirit and approach is that the objects and concepts of science henceforth become, for Weber, 'indelibly marked by a certain *duplicity*' (*II*, xii). No longer distinguished, expressed and regulated by a notion of adequation, the scientific object and the scientific concept undergo processes of interaction and exchange now characterized by much less stable effects of doubleness and ambivalence. Denied grounding in a traditionally conceived order of being and cognition, the more relativistic and experimental science of today therefore concerns itself with securing improvements in the rules of scientific inquiry, forming the basis of a possibility of consensual agreement among the scientific community with regard to provisional truths. Thus, 'the only "intrinsic" support of science is its movement' towards futurity, 'impelling it "to break with its own frames" in order to approach the enigmatic "objects" it addresses' (*II*, xiv). This movement is, necessarily, both a movement towards alterity, towards that which exists outside the realm of scientific knowledge and understanding (an alterity that to a certain extent must be preserved in order to reinforce the sense of ambiguity which, paradoxically, gives definition to the new spirit of relativistic and experimental science); and also, in the very wish to modify so as to improve the 'truth-potential' of formations of knowledge, a movement *against* alterity or the 'unknown'. In other words, the new scientific spirit constitutes itself according to ambivalent processes both of exclusion and inclusion where the 'objects' and thinking of science are concerned.

Perhaps most significantly, since the objects in which science is now interested 'hardly check the centrifugal spin' set off by new discoveries and approaches 'for the very reasons that render it absurd to speak of "objects *themselves*"' (*II*, xiv), the function of establishing identities and imposing determinations so as to secure even the most provisional knowledge with regard to scientific phenomena can only be the effect of 'institutionalization': that is, the effect of procedures, decisions and results that are institutional rather than 'natural' or 'objective', institut*ed* rather than given on condition of a prior reality. Because science cannot be purely scientific according to an adequation conception of truth, the 'operations of science ... entail a relation to alterity that can no longer be considered to be purely intrascientific' (*II*, xiii). For Weber, these operations – neither purely scientific or scientifically self-grounded, nor able to justify themselves according to a demonstrable and separable reality 'outside' of, and prior to, scientific knowledge – are therefore always characterized by interpretive friction and anxiety, in so far as the new scientific spirit stages a turbulent encounter between the ambiguous standing of scientific knowledge and the play of conflictual forces (ones that can never be exclusively scientific) surrounding the ambivalent attempt both to recognize and overcome such ambiguity.

Interpretation and Institution

Moving beyond specific questions of scientific determination and legitimation, Weber in another essay, 'Closure and Exclusion', pursues more widely the often complex, problematic and agonized relationships between institution and interpretation by way of a reading of texts by Nietzsche, Peirce, Saussure and Derrida. Here, Weber takes as his starting-point Derrida's famous discussion, in 'Structure, Sign, and Play in the Discourse of the Human Sciences', of the two most common interpretations of interpretation. According to one version, interpretation is a matter of skilfully deciphering truth or discovering origin, and thus entails foundational or referential thinking, again in terms of a concept of 'adequation'. According to another kind of approach (the one that is usually associated in discussions of 'Structure, Sign, and Play' with Nietzsche and in turn Derrida himself), interpretation is associated with the liberational affirmation of interpretive 'play'. Weber is quick to point out, however, that 'having stated the alternative, Derrida goes on to suggest that what is required is not so much a choice, embracing one at the expense of the other, but rather a reflection upon the "common ground" ... of the two absolutely irreconcilable modes of interpretation' (CE, 4). At the very least, these two apparently incommensurable modes nevertheless relate to, or correspond with, each other in so far as they (in Weber's translation of Derrida) 'divide up the field of the human sciences *among themselves*' (CE, 4), therefore *engaging* in a struggle for dominance within the same, conflictually-riven, territory.

Hence, 'beyond the "irreducible difference" ' of what can be termed 'nostalgic and affirmative interpretations', there lies a third interpretation of interpretation relating (to) the other two: 'interpretation as a struggle to overwhelm and dislodge an already existing, dominant interpretation' (CE, 4–5). This game of war and struggle for interpretive dominance, as well as posing a threat to the 'one' from the 'other', is nevertheless always self-jeopardizing, since actually achieving an overwhelming dominance in the field of interpretation would in fact end interpretation altogether. Hence, in 'Homer's Contests', Nietzsche shows how the Greeks 'sought to safeguard the "necessity of competition"' against itself' (CE, 5) by expelling and excluding excessively dominant competitors from the competition. 'The gesture of *exclusion*', suggests Weber, 'thus emerges as a necessary move designed to save the agonistic process from its own tendencies toward entropy' (CE, 5). However, this move can never simply be assumed to be innocently executed in service of the higher value set upon competition itself (a value that might be thought to transcend competing interests), since the question always arises: who decides on the exclusion of the 'dominant' (indeed, who decides on what constitutes 'dominance') if not those already in some kind of dominant position?

In Nietzsche's essay, then, 'play' is never innocently affirmative or joyous, but always riven with effects of power, struggle and conflict. Moreover, these effects can never simply be attributed to, and understood in terms of, a straightforward logic of incommensurability, confrontation and opposition (a logic that would merely state as 'alternatives' the two modes of interpretation), since the agonistic and conflictual processes of interpretation, characterized by ambivalent patterns of exclusion and (re)inclusion with regard to dominant elements, are instituted as a condition of the game itself (*it-self* – self as double, other than itself).

Weber rearticulates and develops Derrida's suggestion that the two kinds of interpretation remain bound, linked, forever wrestling, within a third 'obscure economy' of interpretation, by way of a reading of Saussure. According to Saussure, the game of language and significa-tion, understood systematically, operates by means of the structuring of differential values and relations determined by 'milieu': that is, the differential value of a sign is determined not by what it represents but by its differential relationship to other signs, or to its linguistic surroundings. But what determines 'milieu'? As Weber puts it, 'if the value of a term is a function of its "pure difference" from "other terms of the system", what determines those other terms as a *system*' (CE, 6), thus arbitrarily, restrictively delimiting (that is, systematizing) the play of pure difference on which, contradictorily, we suppose the system to be based? To put it another way, 'no single signifier or signified can be determined apart from the play of difference, but that play itself must be limited in order for determination to take place' (CE, 6). Here, then, in the vicinity of interpretation's interpretation (by Saussurian linguistics, that is), the affirmation of free play awkwardly contends with an idea of the determinable contexts and systematic structure of meaning – or, in other words, its *institution*. This happens, however, not by way of an explicitly fractious, directly oppositional, utterly self-confounding interchange, but according to a somewhat mobile 'obscure economy'.

The rhythms of this 'obscure economy' might indeed call to mind the two-step movement of 'walking on two feet', a motif that becomes important during Derrida's discussion of the founding and orientation of the university institution in 'Mochlos', an essay that is in turn organized around a close reading of Kant's *The Conflict of the Faculties*. I will discuss this motif more fully towards the end of this chapter, where it becomes pertinent to Weber's discussion of the future and performativity of the humanities, but it is interesting to note here that the movement performed by the processes of institution in Weber's account of Saussurian linguistics already begins to suggest a two-footed motion that propels itself forward only as a species of rather agonized, repetitious activity. Thus, the competitive rivalry between linguistic terms seeking pure differentiation from one another must be circumscribed and delimited by a dominant power (a system) that is nevertheless partially effaced in order that the 'competition' (pure differential play) continues to thrive – which, of course, in the Saussurian economy it can do only as a rule-bound 'system', hence only the *partial* effacement of a dominant constituent among the play of pure differences.

In order to somewhat stabilize this 'obscure economy' of the linguistic system or institution, Weber shows how Saussure feels compelled to introduce and maintain a neat parallelism in the form of a supposedly stable, or at least relatively fixable, structural opposition between signifier and signified, thus arresting the play of pure difference supposed to be at the heart of the signifying process. However, the 'obscure economy' of conflictual interpretations of interpretation, or of the agonistic processes of signification, is not so easily steadied, as Weber goes on to demonstrate via a discussion of the relationships between synchronic and diachronic perspectives within Saussurian linguistics. As is often suggested, Saussure can be thought to privilege the synchronic dimension of the signifying process over the diachronic, in order to present us with a language system that, at any given moment (conceived as a frozen 'momentary state'), is more or less closed and restricted (not least with regard to the linguistic debris of historical process) such that the play of differences between constitutive elements remains intelligible in terms of a determined and determinable 'milieu' or an unshifting, synchronic linguistical environment. On this view, the attempt by Saussurian linguistics to exclude the diachronic dimension in any understanding or comprehension of the linguistic system therefore stems from a polarized way of thinking which leads to the expulsion of that which is imagined to exist 'outside' the functioning of the system itself. Not unlike the repositioning of the signifier and signified as parallel terms stably fixed within a structural opposition, this ostensibly clear-cut antithetical relation between synchrony and diachrony to some extent serves as 'a defense against the unsettling implications of [Saussure's] principle of pure difference' (CE, 9).

However, Weber reminds us that, for Saussure, the linguistic system or institution is upheld not simply because of synchronicity, but more complexly also because of the *perception* of synchronicity among the linguistic community. As Weber puts it, the basis of language's functioning from a Saussurian perspective 'is not simply empirical, since Saussure understood very well that the notion of a "momentary state" of language was a construction, a heuristic fiction' (CE, 7). Crucially, this fiction is not just the product of the linguist's imagination, but – in order for language in general to function at all – it stems from an 'identical collective consciousness' (CE, 7). Now, though, the 'identification of "a system of pure values determined by nothing outside of the momentary state of its terms"' becomes 'curiously dependent on something outside the momentary state of its terms', something not purely linguistic at all (CE, 7). Once again, on closer inspection the Saussurian interpretation of interpretation reveals itself as an 'obscure economy' of agonized (in)determination, thus formed from the inextricable interplay and conflicted struggle between two interpretations of interpretation.

The Habits of a Professional Culture

To suggest that determination is agonized, frustrated and unfulfilled in this way is not, for Weber, to say that it is simply impossible. On the contrary, Weber concurs with what he takes to be one of the main thrusts of the work of the American semiotician Charles Sanders Peirce, that 'despite the tendency of semiotic processes to be open-ended and relatively indeterminate, determination takes place all the time' (LP, 20). Weber's concern, in his essay 'The Limits of Professionalism', is therefore to shift attention within deconstruction from an interest in the aporetic 'conditions of possibility and impossibility' underlying the founding of systems to the more pragmatic question of 'the conditions of *imposability*' that enable them nevertheless to effect and maintain a certain degree of institutionality, however fraught it may be (LP, 19). As Weber notes, 'Peirce's critique of Descartes ... asserts that absolute doubt is make-believe, a fiction of the ego designed to establish its self-identity' (LP, 20) whereas, for Peirce, a state of mind is established not by entirely divesting the mind of content, as Descartes would have it, and thereby reflecting on the pure process of thought or representation *as such*, but instead by engaging in a process of interpretation which, since it arises in the vicinity of pragmatically yet provisionally arranged local determinations, can never be intrinsically stable and therefore 'can only involve an exercise of force, even violence, in order to arrest the inherent tendency of signs to refer to other signs, *ad infinitum*' (LP, 20). On this view, human experience is never simply the experience of a given state of affairs. Rather, it is a matter of struggling – in an inherently conflictual environment – to build interpretive defences against the 'violent shock' of surprise, the trauma of the unexpected or unknown. As far as Peirce is concerned, 'the problem then becomes that of defining the conditions under which such a violent arrestation – in other words: institution – takes place' (LP, 21).

Weber shows how Peirce develops a notion of 'habit' as that which 'limits and delimits the process of thought and interpretation' (LP, 21). Thought, according to Peirce, is basically habit-forming. It constitutes an attempt to achieve control – especially self-control – by means of the cultivation of habits that help us confront (even anticipate) emergencies with an already devised set of responses. However, Weber is quick to point out that this conception of thought powerfully unsettles Peirce's avowed ideal of an academic community engaged in disinterested inquiry since, according to his own assertions, all thought (characterized by the formation of habit) must be *self*-interested. Peirce's strong condemnation of the self-serving practices characterizing the American university system of his day might therefore be interpreted not so much as an insistent attack on anomalies and abuses, but as a mixture of denial on the one hand, and unwitting recognition on the other, that such practices 'might be the inevitable consequence of what Peirce himself saw as the essence of thought: the effort to cope with reality and to maintain self-control' (LP, 23).

This effort gives rise to an academic environment that, following Burton Bleidstein, Weber associates with a long-standing 'culture of professionalism' (LP, 25).[2] Here, the 'set of learned values' identified with the academy's culture turn out to be little more than 'a set of habitual *responses*' designed to serve the interests of self-preservation and self-command. Traditional ideas of academic sovereignty and autonomy reflect not simply the specialism or specialization involved in different academic fields, but more fundamentally translate a sense of the incommensurability of academic production, whereby no standard of equivalence can be introduced to economically calculate or commodify the exchange of the academic profession's services. Such services are thus assigned a value irreducible to the determinations of the market, relating instead to 'a body of systematic, esoteric knowledge' (that is, a discipline) occupying 'a coherent, integral, and self-contained domain' that can be taken as 'reposing on founding *principles*'. This, by implication, suggests a relation of adequation to 'an equally self-contained "natural" state of things' (LP, 25–27).

Such an academic set-up is, of course, increasingly felt to be untenable with the emergence during the twentieth century of new (often interdisciplinary) perspectives and approaches, both in the sciences and the humanities, that render problematic the traditional standing of an 'adequation' conception of truth, as well as being strongly threatened by the commodification of knowledge-exchange that signals the repositioning of the contemporary commercial university in relation to the globalized demands of what has been called 'late' capitalism. To this extent, Weber's remarks on the culture of professionalism may now seem rather outdated. I would argue to the contrary, however. It is precisely here that Weber's ideas remain relevant and require keen re-evaluation in light of the contemporary situation of the university. Despite – indeed, perhaps because of – the impossibly outmoded disciplinary nature of traditional academic culture (given the movement of knowledge outlined in Weber's introduction to *Institution and Interpretation*), a whole host of attempts currently abound to defend such a culture, to preserve the intactness of its ensemble of notions of sovereignty, autonomy and incommensurable value. Such attempts might be taken, on the basis of Weber's account, to reflect a renewed effort to assert or impose (self-)control in the face of 'violent shock'. Indeed, some of the most strongly characteristic features of today's academic scene can be interpreted in this way. For example, many academic departments in the UK effectively colluded with the threat posed to innovative and challenging interdisciplinary projects during the 1990s by the Research Assessment Exercise. While, in practice, the RAE often encourages groupings of academic researchers within any given university setting which remain rather temporary and strategic, the RAE itself supposedly takes the *discipline* as the unit of assessment, and – inasmuch as it subjects knowledge to a marketplace of relational values – primarily establishes a ratio between different university departments *within* the same discipline rather than between the disciplines themselves. In the field of English literature (a field always embattled by debates about the disciplinary value and standing of its activities), this collusion resulted, during the 1990s, in many newly advertised posts demanding expertise in the more traditional disciplinary undertaking of period-based study, such that recruitment was done rather cynically to ensure coverage in research terms of the various periods that, as is frequently supposed, go to make up the content of English literature's 'coherent, integrated, and self-contained domain'. (Again, as many of us will be aware, such developments entail processes of determination, containment and inclusion that simultaneously activate rather forceful processes of (de)limitation, exclusion, expulsion and defence.) In the face of an increasing commodification of academic knowledge-exchange, according to which intellectual output is exposed to the future possibility and threat of commensurability and, thereby, competition within a marketplace of entirely relational values (a wholly 'economic' economy), the stealthy reversion to traditional sorts of disciplinary scholarship might be taken as symptomatic of a nostalgic wish to seek protection within departments that remain more or less isolated (not least, in a Freudian sense) and self-contained. Such departments, once established, can – *as a matter of habit* – increasingly disregard the question of the forcefully instituted limits and limitations going to make up their disciplinary set-up, in favour of an endless, internal regression – a regression that justifies its fixated fascination with 'objects', problems and questions that are imagined to reside solely *within* the field by reasserting traditional discourses of academic seriousness and competence.

Nevertheless, since they are devised primarily as defence mechanisms, such habits will always, at some level, continue to articulate themselves in thoroughly formulaic and repetitious ways to the 'violent shock' of that which they (must) oppose and deny. Hence the manner in which their proponents (in the pages of publications such as the *Times Higher Education Supplement*, for example) *habitually* fret or brood over alternative – one might say, supposedly less adequate(d) – ways of thinking, writing and researching, with a strange combination of obsessional interest and disgust. Here, again, the demarcation of academic fields and disciplines so vital to the academy's professionalized culture involves processes of interpretation that are agonized and conflicted through and through. The anxious mixture of regard and disregard paid to 'postmodernism', 'poststructuralism', 'theory' or 'deconstruction' (among other convenient and habitual labels) might even be explained in terms of a sense of guilt that tenaciously attends the fraught institutionality of the culture's imposed determinations; determinations which – like the value of a linguistic term – must always derive from a formative relationship (albeit a forcefully restrained and restricted one) to other constitutive elements that nevertheless supposedly remain 'outside' their identity. As Weber puts it, albeit in a different context, 'it is precisely the agonistic character of interpretation that necessarily transforms indebtedness into guilt, since the self-affirmation of any interpretation ... can only prevail and impose itself by denying its constitutive dependence on what it excludes, dethrones, and replaces' (DC, 38).

The Ambivalent Institution of the Humanities

This focus on the conflicted relations of exclusion and inclusion that crop up in the vicinity of (the) institution persists in Weber's discussion of the institutional field of the humanities. In another essay, 'Ambivalence: The Humanities and The Study of Literature', he concentrates more specifically on the institutional set-up of the academy in so far as, for many, it has relied historically on a set of distinctions between the arts and the sciences. C.P. Snow's delineation of 'two cultures' is perhaps the most familiar articulation of this idea, although Weber chooses other examples. In R.S. Crane's famous series of lectures, *The Idea of the Humanities*, for instance, it is suggested that the tendency of the sciences to comprehend particular objects and phenomena in terms of their relationship to generalizable paradigms or formulae can be distinguished from the goal of the humanities whereby 'the multiplicity and diversity of human achievements' is underscored in order to celebrate 'uniqueness, unexpectedness, complexity' in arts and letters (cited in A, 136).[3] However, as Weber points out, the very fact that the humanities is, at some level, always bound to institute itself as 'a coherent, integrated, and self-contained domain' of knowledge-practices means that the processes of cognition that take place under its auspices inevitably tend to encourage generalizations. These occur, in order to relate and appropriate individual instances, problems and forms to more universalized sets of propositions and assumptions that are in fact required by the 'humanities' to constitute and delimit a frame of reference (for example, a 'field' or 'discipline') that is, in turn, always needed to enable any sort of – institutionalizable – cognition of even the most singular 'objects'. Here, the *de jure* distinction between the sciences and the humanities starts, *de facto*, to fray at the edges.

In the historically more recent report of the Rockerfeller Commission, *The Humanities in America*, meanwhile, this differentiation of the humanities and the sciences is reworked (with its terms being reversed to some extent) to suggest that, whereas the sciences generally operate by means of isolating, specifying, or in other words systematically excluding their objects of study in order to find proofs and determine laws, the humanities tend to foster 'progressively inclusionary acts' (cited in A, 137).[4] Such 'inclusionary' tactics must nevertheless involve processes of selection and, subsequently, of modification and redefinition of the institutional field, which inevitably necessitate certain delimitations, demarcations and exclusions. As the humanities' tendency towards inclusivity is overwritten as a species of exclusionary activity that is otherwise associated with scientific practice, the 'natural' or conceptual distinctions between the humanities and the sciences once again begin to falter and collapse, and therefore become sustainable only by way of the very conflicted operations of institutionalization itself.

If the *imposed* determination of the characteristic features of the humanities nevertheless relates to an idea of humanistic knowledge of the irreducibly particular, Weber returns to the question of how this can be possible, given the inescapable necessity of repetition and generalization that facilitates cognition or knowledge itself. Here, Weber embarks on a reading of Kant's *Critique of Judgement*. Kant distinguishes between determinant judgement – whereby universal laws, principles or criteria already at our disposal serve to determine knowledge of a particular object – and reflective judgement wherein, more enigmatically, the law followed 'in moving from the particular to the general is based not on the object as such – for, in the absence of a given concept, this is precisely what must be determined – but rather on a relation of the subject to itself' (A, 139). Weber shows how the humanities, as a site of individual and collective human self-reflection, foster precisely this kind of reflective judgement, although, as he points out, 'to see one's mirror image and to arrive at self-knowledge are, needless to say, not necessarily identical' (A, 140), since the inextricable complicity of the subject in the projection and designation of the object (and, perhaps, vice versa) often puts into play complex processes that frequently inhibit, rather than promote, self-evidence or self-reflexive transparency.

However, returning to Kant, Weber notes that the concept of reflective judgement was initially introduced to address a 'situation in the experimental sciences' (A, 140). This suggests that the need felt by Kant for a theory of reflective judgement exposes the extent to which 'the opposition of the humanities and sciences may in fact be less pertinent than their underlying common effort to apprehend the particular and to make it the substance or object of a judgement' (A, 140). From this point of view, reflective judgement becomes an exemplary term (although not always a very obliging one!) in discerning or pursuing the relationship of thought to cognition generally.

The exemplarity of this term is, for Kant, perhaps most pronounced in aesthetic evaluations which, more than any other, seem to perplex an 'adequation' conception of truth or a determinant notion of judgement. And since reflective judgement is both exemplary with regard to aesthetic evaluation in particular and critical to 'an underlying common effort' (A, 140) to reconcile apprehension, cognition and judgement within the field of knowledge generally, Weber suggests that:

> Kant's critical philosophy bequeaths to the modern discipline of literary studies ... a fateful and ambiguous legacy. Literary and aesthetic judgments are assigned a decisive position within all the cognitive activities, inasmuch as such evaluations appear to be exemplary instances of the judgmental process as such .... And yet at the same time aesthetic judgments provide no 'knowledge of its objects' ... and hence they cannot themselves be made the content of any substantive theory or discipline ... In short, the very dignity and significance of the aesthetic judgment as one in which the singularity of the object resists all attempts to subsume it under general concepts also precludes the establishment of a discipline of literary studies or of literary criticism. (A, 141)

While the aporetical project of the humanities (epitomized by literary study) – that of *imparting* the *particular* – may well preclude the robust delimitation of a disciplinary field (at least, inasmuch as such a thing might be defined according to the terms and requirements of a culture of professionalism), nevertheless it is important to recognize that the reflective judgements exemplifying humanistic endeavours within the domain of knowledge do leave traces of very specific – and rather stubborn – kinds. The findings of those in the humanities may not be directly replicable or easily translatable with reference to universal principles or laws, but they are *iterable* nonetheless. Iterability of the kind that stems from reflective judgement entails, at the very least, a re-cognition and therefore a repetition of the 'object' which nevertheless also involves alteration – both of the object and the subject – rather than straightforward reinscription or recurrence.[5] Hence, while a Kantian 'science of the beautiful' will always tend to objectify and effectively immobilize the singular instances of beauty that, notwithstanding, it wishes to celebrate and preserve, any attempted effacement of these tendencies that might stem from a reiteration of the humanities' ideal could never merely de-institute its past, present and future activities. On the contrary, any such supposedly self-effacing reiteration, rather than simply obliterating the traces of iterability (repetition-alteration) already deposited, sedimented and instituted by humanistic inquiry, would necessarily confirm the always *alterable* articulation of the object (in a multiple sense) of the humanities, thus adding to, and partaking of, the very effects of iterability supposedly being effaced. Such recursive effects of continually altering iterability thus do not so much militate against an institutionalizable field of the humanities but, in a sense, define its institution. This irreducible (and somewhat antagonistic) interplay between the supposedly uninstitutionalizable source of the humanities' identity and the recursive iterability of its institution (as perhaps nothing other than iterability) – both of which are linked to the exemplarity of reflective judgement – suggests, once more, the unstable and ambivalent effects of demarcation that attend the very *idea* of the humanities.

Weber therefore advocates institutions that might *assume*, rather than repress, the effects of ambivalence which attend their institution and, indeed, he attempts to envisage possibilities for such institutions. This sets up one in a series of points of contact with Freud, as Weber – exploring such possibilities – suggests that the taboo partakes of ambivalence (that is, of the vexed relation of identity to the other) in more felicitous ways than the neurotic can ever do. He writes: 'Whereas the neurotic's concern for the other conceals an incapacity to accept the other's alterity (and to assume one's own aggressive drives), the "egoistic" attitude provoked by the violation of the taboo ... is in fact more social in its assumption of the otherness of the other' (A, 149). Within the structure, formation and transgression of the taboo, this 'other' is not taken primarily as an ego (or alter-ego) which acts – often vexatiously – as the receptacle for the projection of one's own (aggressive) neurotic drives, discontents and desires. Instead, the 'other' can be found 'acting in the name of a transgressive desire' that is dangerous to the community, so as to receive punishment only at the point where property rights are violated, 'only when transgression seeks to become appropriation' (A, 149) – that is, when the other seeks to appropriate the properties of another or, in effect, tries to 'become the same'. And yet amid this respect for alterity encoded in the rites of punishment, we find 'the socializing force of the taboo' (A, 149), since transgressive desire isn't just felt or executed by the arrogant violator but suggests a possibility that threatens and therefore binds the entire community. Thus ambivalence (the vexed relation of otherness to identity) is assumed and deployed in the structure of the taboo in ways which express and preserve the alterity of the other, paradoxically, at the origins of social bonds.

When this account of taboo rituals is taken in conjunction with Weber's demonstration that Kantian reflective judgement facilitates cognition with regard to irreducibly specific instances only insofar as 'we treat singularities *we* do not understand as though they were products of *another* understanding' (A, 150), we are exposed to a powerful suggestion: that to assume and partake of the effects of ambivalence transforms knowledge into spectacle or, in effect, theatre.

The Future of the University Today

What, then, of more recent contributions by Weber to the question of (the) institution? How do they connect to, and draw upon, his earlier writings, collected together in the original edition of *Institution and Intepretation*? What kinds of insight do they offer concerning both the contemporary situation of the university as described by critics today (Bill Readings in particular) and the possibilities for rereading a body of work on the question of the institution produced in the last two decades by one of the West's most important, although perhaps undervalued, theoreticians?

In a further essay on 'The Future of the University: The Cutting Edge', first published in 1996 by the Research Institute for the Humanities and Social Sciences at the University of Sydney as part of a collection on *Ideas of the University*, Weber offers his response to Bill Readings' study of today's highly commercialized academic institutions. Readings' thesis is, it is difficult to deny, a powerful one. He begins with an historical survey of models of the university after the Enlightenment, showing how the German Idealists from Schiller to Humboldt substituted a concept and a content of culture for Kant's notion of reason as the regulatory ideal of the modern university and the *ratio* between disciplines. In this way, he suggests, they assigned a more explicitly political role to the modern university as the unifying institution in which the sum of knowledge and the cultivation of character (*Bildung*) were tied to the development of the ideological lineaments of modern nation-states. In Germany, in particular, this shift from reason to culture in the formation of the modern university provided a way of reconciling, as Readings puts it, 'ethnic tradition and statist rationality' (*UR*, 15), so as to overcome the otherwise potentially menacing interplay between reason and republican will in the institutional model derived from Kantian thought, while at the same time establishing the conditions to realize the essence of *Volk* in the very plan of the university. The forms of cultural identity cemented via the interplay of university and nation-state from the late nineteenth century onwards in Britain, however, depended on literature rather than philosophy. An 'organic vision of the possibility of a unified national culture' (*UR*, 16) was, as Readings shows, tied to the idea of a canonized national literature, both to stave off the perceived threat of urban, industrial anarchy and social fragmentation from the time of Matthew Arnold onwards and to rebuild and revivify nationhood and national values in the aftermath of two world wars during the twentieth century.

Nevertheless, for Readings, as the ideological apparatus of the nation-state weakens in view of the apparently irresistible rise of transnational corporations with their ideologically 'colourless' logics and practices of managerial excellence, the picture changes decisively within and across various national models of the university. Once the subject of university pedagogy (the student) ceases to be imagined as metonymically the embodiment of generalized social, national or ethnic values (now seen to be in decline in an age of global capital) the 'post-historical' university faces a legitimation crisis which, Readings suggests, it tries to disregard by embracing corporate-style management and bureaucratic rationality, now thinking of itself as simply a business needing to compete among others. Here, the university becomes 'dereferentialized' in relation to any Idea (of reason or culture, nation or ethnicity, for example) such that, as a certain notion of pure performativity takes hold, the actual content of university activity loses importance. Hence, the kind of language that flows from, and indeed structures, a variety of university activities in the contemporary setting frequently revolves around an appeal to a particular idea of 'excellence' borrowed from the realm of private business.

Weber is therefore primarily concerned to take a closer look at the way in which Readings presents the concept and practice of corporate-style 'excellence' as a characterizing feature of contemporary academic institutions. As Readings puts it, in a passage quoted by Weber (FU, 227):

The appeal to excellence marks the fact that there is no longer any idea of the University, or rather that the idea has lost all content. As a non-referential unit of value entirely internal to the system, excellence marks nothing more than the moment of technology's self-reflection. All that the system requires is for activity to take place, and the empty notion of excellence refers to nothing other than the optimal input/output ratio in matters of information. (*UR*, 39)

Here, Weber detects a possible contradiction. Doesn't the self-reflection implied in the movement and measure of excellence – albeit of an apparently extreme technocratic and bureaucratic kind – nevertheless constitute a sort of reference? Perhaps even an exemplary (one might say, historic) sort of self-reference that we might associate with the Enlightenment rather than with the supposedly 'post-historical' present? Weber goes so far as to relate the formation of 'excellence' described by Readings to the determination of the Cartesian cogito itself (a spectre that here returns from his earlier discussion of the work of Charles Sanders Peirce); thereby suggesting that the supposedly 'posthistorical', 'postmodern', 'dereferentialized' university which emerges from the pages of *The University in Ruins* in fact merely repeats and reinscribes characteristically *modern* processes and formations of knowledge, representation, reference and self-identity:

Excellence, like the Cartesian cogito, distinguishes itself from all others, above all from the objects of its representations. It divests itself of all 'content' in order thereby to demarcate its own self-identity, henceforth to be determined in nothing but *the process of representing as such*, which is to say, in the process of 'doubting' as opposed to the determination of that which is doubted. As its name suggests, 'doubting' is *duplicitous*. It doubles and splits itself off from what it doubts and, in so doing, establishes a purely formal relation to its own 'performance.' The grounding force of the Cartesian *cogito*, by which it attains *certitude*, resides in precisely this doubling, splitting and demarcating movement, which produces a kind of pure performativity not so very different from that ascribed by Readings to the notion of 'excellence.' (FU, 231)

On Weber's view, it is as though Readings, in his attempt to apprehend the distinctiveness of the contemporary university, in fact unwittingly repeats the usual, archaic tendency of viewing the university as an institution that is – *and will have remained* – essentially self-grounded and self-contained, even after (and even despite) processes of demarcation that suggest the duplicity of such an image or idea of the university. Far from exposing and confirming the radical transformations undergone by academic institutions in recent times, Readings might therefore actually be seen to resort to habitual thinking as a defence against the violent shock of change, so that the picture of the self-interested university of today he presents us with in *The University in Ruins* may in fact amount to an unwitting projection and preservation of his own academic self-interest. That this response to Bill Readings' book draws upon and reanimates Weber's earlier comments on the culture of professionalism is plain to see. However, to fully recognize this connection powerfully underlines the possibility that, despite Readings' persistent warnings against deploying the rhetoric of denunciation or nostalgia with regard to recent trends in the university, and despite his scepticism about resorting to the language of the discipline or of academic standards in order to mount a defence of traditional knowledge today, Readings himself might just turn out to be – even in his most challenging moments – a creature of habit, at least so far as his account of the university goes. According to this perspective, one might even say perhaps that Readings' continual, albeit rather enigmatic, appeal to (or for) the persistence of 'Thought' in today's university suggests a not-so-obscure echo of Descartes.

While Weber's response to Readings' thesis is highly suggestive and penetrating, however, there might be other ways of reading *The University in Ruins*. Weber concentrates on Readings' notion that the university of excellence is dereferentialized with respect to any content, and therefore that it simply constitutes the moment of 'technology's self-reflection', in order to argue that Readings unwittingly reinscribes an image of the institution as self-reflexive, self-grounded and self-contained, thus embodying the very same formations we associate with Cartesian thought. Nevertheless, it is also possible to view the university of excellence, as described by Readings, in a rather different way – one which, on the contrary, emphasizes the more radically uncertain forms of doubleness, ambivalence and non-self-identicality potentialized by today's academic institutions. Here, by very dint of his argument, Readings would perhaps downplay Weber's emphasis on the tradition-ally isolated standing of academic departments, however conflictually riven their processes of differentiation may be, in favour of a different kind of description of the decline of communicability between disciplines. This description entails a vision not only of disciplinary regression but also of new possibilities and forms of academic community.

According to Readings, the era of 'excellence' signals the decline of notions of communicative transparency and unified community in the university, as advocated by the German Idealists. Such notions become untenable even though the 'generalized spirit of performativity' (Lyotard) supposedly characterizing excellence installs a strong principle of translatability. This paradox occurs, on Readings' account, because the traditional concepts and paradigms of identity and unity that fashion the individual as expression of the institution and in turn the nation-state, or the discipline as expression of the general advancement of knowledge, are irredeemably eroded. As the ideal of

a communicative community wanes along with the expressivist
conception of the relationships between individual, institution and
state, discipline and university, Readings envisages the (perhaps
necessary) possibility of a 'community of dissensus'. This dissensual
community, 'thinking without identity' (*UR*, 127) and thus finding its
very conditions of possibility in the 'excellent' university, would
nevertheless, in practical terms, remain unaccountable with regard to
the institutional logics and practices of accounting, audit, quality
control and so on, that typify the bureaucratic and managerial exercise
of excellence. While this dissensual community could only be spawned
by the 'excellent' university, then its temporality would be entirely
incompatible with today's auditing or monitoring devices and performance indicators precisely because 'thinking without identity' would
necessarily be 'systematically incapable of closure' (*UR*, 128) and quite
incomprehensible in terms of the strictly calibrated measure of
excellence. 'Thinking without identity' would, for Readings, *'keep the
question of evaluation open*, a matter of dispute – what Lyotard would
call the differend' (*UR*, 130). By keeping open the question of evaluation
as a condition of 'thinking without identity', the dissensual community
of the 'excellent' university would at every turn transvalue the evaluative
procedures of excellence. It would do so from a 'standpoint' that could
be located neither simply inside nor outside the contemporary
institution. Instead, the dissensual community, 'thinking without
identity', would necessarily mark and re-mark the incommensurability
of the Idea-less university with itself or, to put it another way, would
indicate the rather ungainly two-(left?-)footedness of the institutional
body. This aspect of Readings' book suggests that his analysis of the
ruined university of excellence calls to mind, once again, Derrida's idea
of (affirming) the academic institution as one that 'walks on two feet' (a
motif that we'll return to later on). Here, then, far from re-presenting
today's university in terms of age-old formations of unity and self-
identicality, Readings can be seen to skilfully highlight – and
productively utilize – the highly conflicted and ambivalent effects
consequent upon the dynamic of differentiation required by the very
processes of institutionality. This places him at less of a remove from
Weber than the latter might perhaps imagine.[6]

The Humanities and the Future

In another recent essay, 'The Future of the Humanities: Experimenting',
Weber suggests that self-production of the kind manifested by the
Cartesian cogito, which serves in turn as the basis for a model of
institutionalizable knowledge and representation, finding – for Weber at
least – a somewhat nightmarish completion in Readings' description of

today's university of excellence, also underpins a notion of the 'human' that in fact gives rise to the humanities. Here, then, Weber returns to the question of the humanities that had interested him in his earlier writings. In particular, it is the question of the humanities' future (the future of, for and in, within and in view of, the humanities), addressed rather briefly and somewhat enigmatically toward the end of 'Ambivalence: The Humanities and the Study of Literature', that now takes centre-stage.

'To be "human" came, at least in the modern period, to be synonymous with the power and potentiality of *self-realization*', writes Weber (FH, 236–37). Analogously, humanistic endeavour in universities from the Renaissance onwards tended to establish itself 'at a more or less secure distance from the conflicts of social life' (FH, 238) in the hope of arriving at secure, reliable knowledge as the grounding for humanists' 'own powers and procedures of representation and cognition' (FH, 238). However, the demarcation and separation of the Cartesian ego or of the knowing human 'self' in regard to all forms of externality and otherness would appear to position human cognition (and, by extension, the institutional space of the humanities) in terms of the production and realization of a rather static, always self-identical 'instant' prior to temporal and spatial alteration. This would seem to contradict Weber's earlier insistence, from the perspective of institutionalization, on the always alterable and iterable knowledge-products of the humanities.

However, following Weber, it is important to remember that such a separation of the ground of the 'human' (and of the humanities) as enabling a mode of self-production and self-reflection always requires, in practice, ambivalent strategies of demarcation: not just strategies of exclusion, but also of engagement, of assimilation and inclusion of 'external' elements. Hence, as an institution dedicated to the overcoming of uncertainty, Weber asserts that the modern university was constructed as 'a *model of unification* legitimating the *political containment* of conflictual diversity, whether that of social relations or that involved in historical transformations' (FH, 238). This tied the university to the nation-state as the political institution bound up with the 'manifestation of the *unity* and wholeness of a given society, above and beyond the diversity and often the disunity of its components groups' (FH, 238). The university (as both an idea and, effectively, a set of practices) thus intervened in such conflictual situations, both with regard to particular instances and in more general 'ideological' terms, specifically via the (habitually reiterated) idea of the humanities and of the 'human'. Today, and in the future, we might imagine that the university begins to reclaim and salvage such a role on a global scale by intervening in the conflictual processes underpinning globalization itself, once more to posit (along with other, supposedly 'democratic' Western institutions) a universality – that of the 'human' – which legitimates certain kinds of containment with regard to the effects of globalization's violence (as well as, on occasion, a certain 'complementary', 'necessary' renewal of force).

The unstable and ambivalent processes of exclusion and inclusion that characterize the very formation of the university (and, indeed, the modern humanities) after Enlightenment therefore unsettle its grounding in the supposed determination of the Cartesian cogito as entirely self-actualizing. Such instability and ambivalence must be understood in contexts that are *profoundly* spatial and temporal, especially when one considers the violent histories of modern nation-states in which the university, as a concept and a set of practices, has historically intervened.

Perhaps to deal with this tension between, on the one hand, the apparent self-constitution of the 'human', the humanities and the university and, on the other, the *partiality* of its universal and totalizing claims with respect to others (a theme that preoccupies earlier work), Weber orchestrates a subtle shift of focus from Descartes to Schelling, in order to develop his discussion of the idea of the humanities. At first glance, both would seem to agree that self-knowledge founds the unity and totality of the cogito – for to think is to know that one thinks – or indeed the 'human' (just as the university as a site of self-actualization and self-reflection subsequently provides a universalizable idea of the 'human', in order to counteract conflict and disunity between or within societies and groups). However, at the very beginning of the nineteenth century, when Schelling contemplates the question of method with regard to academic study in the university specifically, he concludes, as Weber puts it, 'that the indispensable *unity* and *totality* so sorely missed by the beginning student can be provided by the University only to the extent that it also *reflects* upon the general conditions under which specific knowledge is possible' (FH, 241). This sounds like a certain kind of Cartesianism, to be sure. Schelling concedes quite explicitly that even empirical truths characteristic of specific or particular knowledge are subject to the generalized conditions of paradigmatic thinking and knowing, recalling for us the problems of aesthetic and determinant judgement in Kant, discussed at length by Weber in the earlier essay on 'Ambivalence'. What Schelling therefore suggests is that, as Weber notes, 'the very process of producing or acquiring cognition may itself be particularly blind to its own conditions of possibility, or impossibility, inasmuch as it tends to take for granted the status of the knowledge it produces' (FH, 241). Schelling's solution to this problem of comprehending hitherto 'unknown' objects only (and of necessity) by means of the existing available apparatuses of knowledge is to posit in idealist terms the essential unity of thinking and being, of the 'unconditionally Ideal and the unconditional Real', so as to found a concept of the 'Absolute' which thereby rests upon their union. Weber tells us that 'the primary characteristic of this "absolute" is already indicated by the etymology of the word: it is *de-tached* and yet at the same time, *self-contained*. In this respect, it can be seen as a continuation of the Cartesian cogito' (FH, 242). But such absolutely detached self-containment in fact tends to problematize and erode the identity of the (self-)knowing subject (and hence, knowledge), since this identity can only be thought to be securely demarcated via a determinable relation to externality, otherness, non-identity. 'In short, the process of separation was so radical [in Schelling] that it tended to undermine the sphere it was introduced to protect: that of the indivisible, self-contained subject' (FH, 242). Hence, at the moment when Western thought pursues a certain version of Cartesianism to an absolute degree, it simultaneously becomes dissatisfied with 'the solution proposed by Descartes: that of an *ego as the unified and indivisible instance* claiming to guarantee the integrity of thought' (FH, 242).

Schelling attempts to overcome this problem of the necessarily 'extended' relation of a (supposedly) self-realizing subject to external phenomena, which in fact allows a differentiation of its identity to occur, by positioning 'man' or the 'human' as the extension and completion of 'the world-appearance'. In so far as 'man' as a rational being is made in the very image of God, he exists as an expression of divinity 'in the Ideal'. Thus 'man' complements and completes the divine revelation which manifests itself in nature only in the 'Real'. Here, then, in a shift away from Cartesianism, the 'human' now provides a 'phenomenal, manifest, visible and sensible *synthesis* of what otherwise would remain radically separated from the world and confined to the realm of the Ideal, to thought rather than to knowledge' (FH, 243). Such a movement would appear to open new horizons and opportunities for knowledge (ones that would have been incompatible with the basic premises of Cartesianism), since 'knowledge presupposes a correlation between thinking and the phenomenal, sensible world' (FH, 243).

Hereafter, therefore, the notion of the 'human' and of the humanities enables *at one and the same time* the extension and the delimitation of the subject of cognition – not least with regard to the field of knowledge thereby opened up – while also creating the basis for an exploration of the relationship between the particular and the universal where 'thinking and the phenomenal' are concerned. For Weber, however, such a thinking of method in and for the humanities exercises only a tenuous and temporary hold, not least with the onset of modern science and the birth of the new scientific spirit, giving rise to an experimental method that in turn begins to characterize the emergence of 'theory' in the humanities. Here, a radical questioning of the possibility of universal claims, full systematicity and synthesis in the field of knowledge encourages a view of both the object and the activity of study as necessarily limited and partial in nature. Thus, over and against the compromise measures developed by thinkers such as Schelling to deal with the implosive tensions of Cartesianism, such an experimental method once again 'radicalizes the Cartesian movement of separation to a point where it no longer can easily serve as the basis for a self-contained subject' (FH, 243). The humanities, as the name for a mode of self-realization and self-fulfilment where the possibility of the 'human' is concerned, thereby gives way to an experience of possibility that is now inextricably bound up with a reflection upon the 'radical and aporetic dynamic of differentation' (FH, 244). Here the name of deconstruction comes to mind for Weber, because it sets against the traditional logic of identity – a logic that might be said to found (but also confound) a certain version of the humanities – a concept of iterability (one which, as we've seen, cannot simply be opposed to the 'humanities'): 'Iterability is necessary because nothing can be recognized as being identical with itself – nothing can be "cognized" – without being first *re*-cognized: that is, without being repeated, compared with its earlier instance, and through that comparison being constituted as self-same' (FH, 245). In (the humanities in) deconstruction, certain kinds of repetition and recurrence – which are themselves both supplementary and originary – return to haunt the Cartesian logic of (self-)identity that inaugurates thought, and, thereafter, knowledge in the tradition of the Enlightenment. Just as the Cartesian cogito attains self-identity via a process of doubling, splitting off and reflection, so the 'other' or the 'double' (that which is, first of all, necessary for *re*-cognition to take place, yet soon conveniently forgotten once the identification of the 'self-same' is completed) returns as an excluded or repressed term – yet, crucially, a constitutive element – of this process, revealing the very movement of demarcation and substitution as one which, in fact, renders problematic any hope or expectation of unity or synthesis. Hence, for Weber:

> The challenge to the humanities ... is to rethink the human in terms of iterability; which is to say, as an effect that is necessarily multiple, divided and never reducible to a single, selfsame essence. The task of the humanities would thus become nothing more or less than that of *rethinking the singular*, which is something very different from subsuming the individual under the general or the particular under the whole. The *singular* is not the *individual*, precisely by virtue of its mode of being, which can never be *simply* that of a once-and-for-all but rather, paradoxically, that of an after-effect of iterability. The singular is that which is left over after the process of iteration has come full circle: it is the remnant or remainder.... . (FH, 245)

This thinking of iterability, which for Weber poses a necessary challenge to the contemporary humanities, is linked to the question of repetition in the philosophical tradition, not least in the work of Kierkegaard and Benjamin. Hence, in 'The Future of the Humanities', iterability and repetition are discussed in a number of contexts: the issue of technological reproducibility and virtualization; the question of a future today; and the theme of the trace of the other, a trace that remains in even the most apparently self-actualizing repetition or re-presentation of the Same (in the media or the university, for instance).

Kierkegaardian experimenting is an undertaking, an iterative venture or movement, which separates itself from, but also in a sense repeats, the experimental method of the sciences. It reactivates the tension in scientific experimentation between, on the one hand, a certain repetition (that is, the attempt to derive replications under controlled circumstances) and, on the other, the non-total, fragmentary character of its findings, in order to iterate a difference within this repetition, so that 'whereas the scientific experiment still seeks to subsume the particular case under the general, and whereas it still situates itself within the confines of a system or at least with respect to systematizable knowledge, the Kierkegaardian experiment is an attempt, a "venture" ... that attempts to articulate the singular (*Enkelte*) *without* entirely dissolving its differences into the similitude of the universal' (FH, 249). This renders the Kierkegaardian experiment, in a sense, both actual and immediate, and also always transitional, unfinishable, ongoing and futural. Moreover, the performative aspect of this experimental articulation of the singular once more raises the question of *theatre*. This echoes Weber's earlier discussion of the always alterable and iterable findings of the humanities, which in 'Ambivalence: The Humanities and the Study of Literature' are seen to generate and reflect effects of ambivalence that he argues might be assumed, rather than repressed, via an exploration of the possibilities of the *theatricality* of the taboo. For Weber, the primarily performative theatricality of the Kierkegaardian experiment as a singular adventure remains irreducible to dramatic narrative of the kind associated with Western theatre since Aristotle. In German, or indeed in Danish, the word for such a theatre is *posse*. In Kierkegaard's essay on repetition, we find a description of one of the leading *posse* actors of his own time, Beckmann. Constantin, Kierkegaard's 'pseudonymic author', remains fascinated with Beckmann's singular style, the performative brilliance of which consists in, as Weber puts it, 'nothing more or less than the way he enters the scene' (FH, 250) – that is, the performance of theatre as an (impossibly) actual and immediate expression of possibility. Constantin comments:

In an art theater proper, one rarely sees an actor who can really walk and stand. As a matter of fact, I have seen only one, but what B. is able to do, I have not seen before. He is not only able to walk, but he is also able to *come walking*. To come walking is something very distinctive, and by means of this genius he also improvises the whole scenic setting. (Cited in FH, 251)[7]

If the humanities (or indeed the concept of the 'human') can no longer provide a forum for the expression of self-identical, self-realizing entities, transcending spatio-temporal considerations and thereby establishing the ground for universal or totalizing claims within the field of knowledge, then for Weber the humanities' future must be tied to this specifically *theatrical* or performative enactment of the singular[8] as the basis nonetheless for an altogether different experience of repetition, captured in the very image of Beckmann walking (as inevitably a repetitious act), and indeed in Constantin's description of it as that which *already is to come* (Beckmann doesn't just begin to walk. The distinctiveness of his '*coming*' relates to the fact that he comes walking already, as it were.[9]) Here, iterability involves a repetition that is singularly not the same, if only because the doubled, fractured temporality implied by the semantic and syntactical structure of this formulation – *already is to come* – ruptures any notion of a self-identical origin or form of the singular. (Paradoxically, this would be what makes the 'singular' absolutely *un*repeatable in a conventional sense.) That the singularity of this experience of repetition is intimately tied to an experience of *iterability*, in the sense given the term by Derrida, suggests that the depiction of Beckmann 'coming walking' might prove very apt with regard to the 'ambivalent' potentiality of the humanities, described more than a decade earlier by Weber in 'Ambivalence: The Humanities and the Study of Literature'.

Walking on Two Feet

Having orchestrated the rather late entrance of Beckmann in order to set the scene of the humanities and the university today, I want to conclude this chapter with some final and necessarily brief remarks, linking – as an invitation to further thought – Weber's and Derrida's evocations of institutional problems, problematics and possibilities. In particular, I want to suggest that the inspiration Weber may well have drawn from Derrida's work on the institution might be apparent in inventive lines of inquiry he has subsequently pursued, which in fact illuminate for us today important aspects, elements and implications of Derrida's work – ones that have perhaps been rather neglected in recent debates concerning the university institution.

The motif of walking that acquires such a strange importance in Weber's recent writing on the institution echoes some of the images and concerns of Derrida's 'Mochlos', a paper originally delivered at Columbia University in 1980. Here, Derrida suggests that the founding of the university is akin to an act of performative force not reducible to a mere 'university event' (M, 29) – just as the founding of the law is not simply a juridical question, one either of 'legality' or 'illegality'. This involves a somewhat uncertain and unstable relationship to alterity, so that, in an important sense, the moment at which (indeed, the *movement by which*) the university finds, founds or foots itself cannot be traced to a single, identifiable instant or point of origin. Like Beckmann, the university 'comes walking'. The leverage that propels the university into being is of a double and perhaps duplicitous nature, a two-footed phenomenon at the very least, as Derrida goes on to imply. Thus the *Idea* of the university as a unified institution purely demarcated by the ideals of reason cannot help but founder on its own foundations. It is thereby beset by a conflict which cannot easily be dismissed as the result of intrusive, external intervention on the part of society or government, nor simply attributed to a wholly *internal* problematic – a planning error or suchlike. Instead, a crisis is suggested, which, according to Derrida's patient exploration of Kant's *The Conflict of the Faculties*, is interminable, giving rise to an aporetical movement that *already is to come*. If 'there can be no pure concept of the university ... due very simply to the fact that the university is *founded*' (M, 29–30), in the face of this deep-seated legitimation crisis Derrida puts these questions. How can we orient ourselves in the university (within, in relation to – the question already faces in and comes from more than one direction)? How does the university orient itself? How exactly does it found, foot and find itself in this aporetical situation? The relationship between these concerns of Derrida's and some of the main thrusts of Weber's work on issues of *institution* and *imposability* should, by now, be very clear.

Through a detailed reading of Kant's *The Conflict of the Faculties*, Derrida suggests that Kant wants to contain and control the damaging and divisive energies of this 'interminable' crisis by insisting on its nature as mere 'conflict' rather than total 'war' (M, 28). The solution he proposes for the university is therefore a 'parliamentary' one, with the institution reconceived as a 'faculty parliament'. On these terms, the higher faculties (theology, law, medicine) take up the right bench and defend the statutes of government, while the left bench is occupied by the philosophy faculty, offering 'rigorous examinations and objections' in the name and pursuit of truth (M, 28). For Kant, the opposition that results from this 'parliamentary solution' serves the higher purposes of a 'free system of government' and therefore resolves conflict into a more fundamental image of balance and unity. Drawing on Kant's 'What is Orientation in Thinking?' however, Derrida points out that 'right' and 'left' are not recognized or classified according to 'a conceptual or logical determination' but only from 'a sensory topology that has to be referred to the subjective position of the human body' (M, 31). This implies that left and right cannot be stably fixed according to incontrovertible logical determinants or wholly objective criteria. Thus, the 'parliamentary' opposition between left and right into which the university's conflicts are extended and ostensibly resolved by Kant offer a no more reliable source of orientation for the university. As Timothy Bahti puts it (in an essay on 'The Injured University' that appears alongside 'Mochlos' in the collection *Logomachia: The Conflict of the Faculties*), 'when we use corporeal directions we mean, "Be like me"' (IU, 62), and therefore we address the other's right as if it were a left, the other's left as if it were a right. The ensuing confusions between my left (side/hand/foot) and another's right potentialized by these circumstances can be situated not just in the subjective position of the human body, but in the sensory orientations collectively of parliamentary members within a body politic of modern, democratic, Western society developing after Kant. Thus, as Bahti points out with regard to certain modern institutions of government, 'in the parliamentary situation, the left – the "opposition" – is located from the perspective of the president or the speaker, but the speaker's left is obviously the left's right' (IU, 62). The left, from this point of view, can only assert its leftness or oppositional stance by way of a (sensory or perceptual) repression of its right side. (Indeed, paradoxically enough, its leftness, and therefore its oppositionality, is only secured because the president or speaker, the overarching figure of authority in this situation, legitimates this reorientation, recasting right as left.)

Such disorientations between left and right suggest an image of an unbalanced body, a body 'off-balance' or suffering imbalance – a body or an institution, like the university, disoriented because it is unsure of its ground, of its very foundations. In such a situation of imbalance, it is difficult to know how to proceed, what direction to take – although the very image of a body 'off-balance' basically suggests the inevitability of movement, the performing of a certain kinetics not reducible to the more static determination (founding?) of a concept or idea. How, then, to proceed? Describing his own experience of receiving treatment for a collapsed left lung, Bahti tells how, in order to restore balance, he was made by his doctors to take up a position in which his body's weight was by means of leverage shifted toward the healthy side (in this case, the right) 'inhibiting the free and strong use of the healthy lung, while forcing the injured side to do more of the breathing while it is also released of its "share" of the body's weight' (IU, 68). This example of leverage, of levering between left and right, sets up a sort of levered relationship with Derrida's essay 'Mochlos' (*mochlos* is a Greek word for 'lever'). In 'Mochlos', it is the leverage between right and left, between newly founded and inherited laws, that in some way allows the body (the human body, the body politic, the body of the university) to walk, as it were, 'on two feet' (M, 31),[10] or, put differently, to 'come walking'. Indeed, the lever (foot) that propels one forward nevertheless roots itself to the spot to do this, thus demanding a serious rethinking of 'newness' or invention, of radicalism and of origination. Such a rethinking would, once again, link the reading of Kant pursued by Derrida in 'Mochlos' (especially regarding the motif of a university 'walking on two feet') to Beckmann's style of performance so admired by Constantin (with the distinctiveness of Beckmann's 'coming' relating to the fact that, theatrically, he comes walking already, as it were). Such a performance, as we have said, proves very apt with regard to the 'ambivalent' potentiality of the humanities, described during the early 1980s by Weber himself. Furthermore, to the extent that Derrida's essay assumes as necessary – not least for its own critical practice – the aporetical movement of founding, footing or *instituting* that it detects throughout *The Conflict of the Faculties*, Derrida's reading of Kant here is not merely descriptive or interpretive, but performative (and, which might be to say a similar thing, *iterable*) through and through. One might even say that this rereading of Derrida's work in light of a detailed survey of Weber's writing on the question of the institution suggests quite profoundly important orientations with regard to the thinking of deconstructive practice itself within and in respect to (its) institutional settings. In turn, such a suggestive rethinking would provide an opportunity to re-evaluate the (institutional) politics of deconstruction beyond the traditional and wearisome theory–practice oppositions, in all its performative dimensions.

As Bahti suggests, therefore, Derrida's insight into the university 'walking on two feet' needs to be treated carefully. In particular, Bahti himself is keen to 'ward off a possible misunderstanding' that might arise with regard to his own discussion of injury and imbalance: namely, the assumption that 'a certain symmetry verging on stasis ... is perhaps being held out as either an original health to be restored, or an ideal state to be attained, or both' (IU, 73). Rather, for Bahti, and implicitly for Derrida, it is a question – especially when discussing the university – of 'recognizing imbalance as the condition within which leverage can and does take place' (IU, 73–74). (The conditions of this imbalance, according to Derrida's reading of Kant, are of course not dissimilar to the kinds of ambivalent demarcations described by Weber over the years, in the context of a number of institutional problems and settings.) This imbalance we have begun to link to an insoluble disorientation between left and right in a university uncertain as to its ground. And such an imbalance imposes and enacts itself, often in spectacularly fraught and tensile ways, through a continual movement, a performance, that we might call leverage.

We are called today, I think, to speculate on such leverage as it takes place. And (in a way that moves both beyond and within the conflicted and unstable demarcations of theory and practice) this must *of necessity* involve the taking of steps – although, of course, Weber's work more generally indicates that this 'taking of steps' may not amount to the realization of voluntary, intentional acts undertaken from an extra-territorial perspective. 'Coming walking', we might well be overtaken – or overcome – by such steps just as we take them.

Notes

1   GREPH stands for Groupe de recherches sur l'enseignement philosophique (Research Group on the Teaching of Philosophy).
2   On the culture of professionalism, see also Samuel Weber's essay, 'The Vaulted Eye: Remarks on Knowledge and Professionalism', *Yale French Studies*, 77 (1990), 44–60.
3   Weber here refers to R.S. Crane's *Idea of the Humanities* (Chicago, IL and London: University of Chicago Press, 1967), 12.
4   Weber here refers to William J. Bennett *et al.*, *The Humanities in America* (Berkeley, Los Angeles and London: University of California Press, 1980), 15.
5   The altering effects of iterability that derive from academic knowledge and practice within the humanities not only relate to a defining moment or instance of judgement in Kantian philosophy. They also resonate strongly with the movement of knowledge, away from the rather static paradigm of adequation and toward a recognition of the more mobile and transformative aspects of cognition. This is a movement that, for Weber, becomes decisive with regard to twentieth-century scientific and intellectual endeavour generally. In this sense, the project of the humanities may well be aporetical but nevertheless remains exemplary (rather than, as is often suggested, becoming increasingly marginal and perhaps even obsolete in relation to the modern university or indeed today's society).
6   See my book *Rethinking the University: Leverage and Deconstruction* (Manchester: Manchester University Press, 1999) especially ch. 3: 'Excellence and Division: The Deconstruction of Institutional Politics', 73–90.
7   The reference here is to Kierkegaard's *Fear and Trembling/Repetition*, ed. and trans. Howard V. Hong and Edna H. Hong (Princeton, NJ: Princeton University Press, 1983), 163.
8   It would be interesting to reflect on the relationship between the pure performativity that Readings, following Lyotard, associates with the late twentieth-century bureaucratic and technocratic university, and the kinds of performativity we might, following Weber, associate with experimentation, *posse-*acting, deconstruction. The differences between these two modes of performativity are in some respects very clear, not least with regard to issues of singularity, repetition and translatability. However, the idea of a straightforward opposition between these two modes of performativity might, I suspect, prove less helpful than a reflection on their common ground, or at least their specific interaction in the context of 'an obscure economy' or, indeed, in terms of Derrida's notion of a university 'walking on two feet'.
9   In the essay's conclusion, Weber appeals to the singular and the exceptional as that which *repeats* separation only to transform and deform it (somewhat along the lines of the experimentation that Bachelard associated with the 'new scientific spirit'). Here, far from guaranteeing the self-identicality of phenomena undergoing isolation, such separation in fact reveals irreducible exceptions that re-mark separation itself 'as a *movement of resistance*' (FH, 252) to synthesis, systematicity, autonomy and totality.

10 The question of the *gait* of the university might perhaps appear to recast important issues concerning the university itself in a rather eccentric or frivolous manner, operating at a certain remove from the more 'sober' and 'serious' discourse of 'proper' academic inquiry. However, since it is the institutional body *in* or *by which* human knowledge in the arts and sciences gains *standing*, the issue of the university's gait might be more fundamental than would otherwise be expected, especially when one considers the following ruminations by Heidegger on the question of technics, to which the next chapter of this book will return. Indeed, in the ensuing quotation, cited in Weber's essay 'Upsetting the Setup' (US, 59–60), what is entailed is not just the question of technological man, but also implicitly a number of long-standing concerns within the various fields of intellectual endeavour, not least philosophy, so that the question of technology turns out to remain inextricably linked with that of knowledge, and indeed *institution*. Heidegger writes: 'man, in midst of beings [*physis*] to which he is exposed [*ausgesetzt*], seeks to gain a stand [*einen Stand zu gewinnen*] and to establish himself, when in the process of mastering beings he proceeds in such and such a way, then this proceeding against beings is supported and guided by a knowledge of beings. This *knowledge* is called *techne*.' (This quote is taken from Martin Heidegger, *Nietzsche*, Bd. I (Pfullingen: Gunther Neske, 1961). The translation is Weber's.) The fundamental stakes involved in 'gaining a stand', both for technological thinking and development and for the philosophical tradition, therefore provide an extremely important context in which to situate Derrida's reading of Kant in his essay, 'Mochlos'.

Chapter 3

The Place of Technics

Technics and Emplacement

In questing after Heidegger's questing after technics, Samuel Weber suggests that technics manifests and determines a sort of consciousness aspiring to certitude, insofar as the endeavour of technics toward 'the unlocking of beings as such' (rather than just the making or producing of particular things) involves an effort 'to control and secure' (US, 70) so as to 'emplace' the beings and the objects with which it is concerned. For Heidegger, therefore, one of the exemplary instances of technics is 'the production and stocking of energy (and of its "raw materials")' (OO, 52). Here, we find an often frantic effort to control, secure, and 'emplace' irreducibly kinetic forces by attempting to determine and delimit them as a 'standing stock' (US, 72). But, of course, the processes of 'controlling', 'securing' and 'emplacing' associated with such technics not only aspire to certainty by way of a frequently forceful exclusion or repression of any 'alternative that cannot be brought before and set into place' (OO, 52) in relation to the calculative rationality of the subject; at the same time, they concern themselves with a way or movement of 'unsecuring' (US, 70), as the art of technics entails the ability to 'dis-lodge' in order to '*re-place*' (OO, 52). The knowledge of technics arising from its attempt to unlock beings as such rests not just on processes of 'emplacement' that can be understood as eventuating ultimately in 'a static state of affairs' (US, 72). Rather, emplacement is itself a continual '*goings-on*' (US, 62), an ongoing and dynamic process which relies on an unavoidable and necessary activity of dis-closing or 'opening up' in order to 'close down' (US, 72) the beings or the objects with which it deals. Technics therefore *places* precisely by putting *place* continually into *play*. Through the somewhat ambivalent and tensile processes of emplacement, then, technics actually 'moves *away* from itself in being what it is' (US, 63) with the result that the essence of technics cannot itself be described as merely 'technical', or even, for that matter, properly 'essential', since 'essence' implies a unified, self-same, irreducible quality or condition that ultimately remains or *stays still* 'in-itself'.

Weber tells us that 'the name' of technics which Heidegger 'assigns to this play' of emplacement is one 'in which the question of determination joins that of institutionalization' (US, 59). We are enjoined, therefore, to consider the question of institution as it forms a join or hinge in regard to the play of technics, and this is a matter to which we will need to return.

The determination of modern technics as described by Heidegger represents, as Weber suggests, a continuation of the project and problematics of subjectivity after Cartesianism. Since the certitude to which technics aspires involves a bringing-before and setting-into-place in regard to the subject, technics is situated:

> ... in relation to the unfolding of subjectivity as the securing of the self ... modern technics thus emerges as the complementary and complicit other and even as the condition of the unconditional and ultimately nihilistic voluntarism that, according to Heidegger, marks the culmination and consummation of modern metaphysics. (OO, 52)

But the way of 'securing the self' after (or in the manner of) Cartesianism actually tends to deobjectify objects, as they become 'increasingly subject to the calculations of a subjective will struggling to realize its representations and thereby to place itself in security' (US, 73). Hence, modern technics once more not only 'emplaces', locates, delimits and produces a knowledge of objects and beings which thereby eventually stay still or remain 'in-themselves' before or over against a subject of cognition. Instead, such technics involve somewhat ironical and perhaps even duplicitous goings-on that cannot help but undermine the stability and security of the very same objects which technics seeks to produce for itself in order to know and to sustain itself. Emplacement's 'unsecuring' in relation to the beings, objects and *places* that it locates, produces and knows means that, finally, there are in fact no secure places; and, indeed, 'the more technics seeks to *place* the subject into safety, the less safe its *places* become' (US, 74). Rather frighteningly, in a variety of contexts concerning modern technology (from industrial and military production to the technologies of modern transportation), this is a goings-on, a *play*, that cannot stop.

Weber's Technics

If technics strives towards a knowledge which unlocks beings as such, then, as Weber remarks, '*techne* is a form of *poiesis* that in turn is closely related to art' (US, 60). Tellingly, Weber's *Mass Mediauras* – as one of his most decisive contributions to the thinking of technics and technologies – itself gets going or gets under way with an essay on 'The Unraveling of Form'. This essay deliberates problems of aesthetic judgement and form in order for the question of technics to be put in the subsequent parts of the book. If, when considering the relation of Weber's work on technics to his other writings, we allow the complex resonance of certain turns of phrase to be heard, we might even say that the issue of 'emplacement' which arises in Weber's more explicit remarks about technics actually *comes into play* or *takes place* in his thinking of aesthetic judgement in relation to the Western philosophical tradition. Tellingly enough, of course, such problems of aesthetic judgement, especially after Kant, have been an abiding interest of Weber's since at least his earlier writing on the question of institution, raising once more the question of where to *place* (not least, in Weber's 'work' itself) the putting into play of (the question of) place which comes to define what is at issue in technics. In fact, to the extent that the 'essence' of 'technics' is neither properly technical nor, indeed, essential, it is no wonder that 'the goings-on of technics find their truth in the displacements that mark the encounter with poetry and with art in general' (US, 75). Such encounters recall and re-pose the ambivalent processes of 'emplacement' not just because of the disputed grounds of canonicity in aesthetics and criticism over the last decades, but also, as we shall see, because of a more originary unravelling of the lineaments and contours of form to be found in Kantian thought almost from the beginning. In 'Upsetting the Setup: Remarks on Heidegger's "Questing after Technics"', Weber concludes his reading of Heidegger's essay by reflecting on this encounter of technics with poetry and art. Here, he states that an 'alternative to the calculations of technical rationality' might be 'a mode of thought' hatched in, and necessitated by, the insterstitial movements and spaces of such displacements, a 'mode' which can therefore 'never be reduced to emplacement or compre-hended in its terms' (US, 75). But in view of the non-technical and non-essential truth of technics, this very mode or manner of thought might not simply propose itself as an 'alternative to the calculations of technical rationality'. Instead, such an 'alternative' might be thought to come into view as the very *condition* of this rationality's ambivalent processes of emplacement and disclosure.

The problem of thinking about where to place a thinking of technics in relation to Weber's work generally is thus foreshadowed or presupposed by the very complex energies and movements of technics which Weber himself describes as a 'goings-on' that in fact exceeds absolute categorization – not least in the sense that such 'goings-on' take place in a way that *re-poses* rather than *resolves* the very question of place. To take this problem further, it is worth deploying an example from Weber's work on the media today. Writing in a way that draws strongly on his engagement with Heidegger's thinking of technics, Weber in 'Television: Set and Screen' reflects on the complex structure of television as *medium*, suggesting that:

> ... the more technology seeks to put things in their proper places, the less proper those places turn out to be, the more displaceable everything becomes and the more frenetic becomes the effort to reassert the propriety of the place as such. If the word 'television' in ordinary usage applies not

just to the medium as a whole but, more precisely, to its materialization as the receiving *set*, this emphasizes just how determining the aspect of 'setting' and 'placing' is for a medium that deprives distance as well as proximity of their traditional stability and hence of their power to orient. (TSS, 124)

How, then, is one to orient an approach to technics – for example, 'in' Weber's 'work' as perhaps its 'medium'? How does technics 'take place' here, or where is one to 'find' it? How, for instance, is one to determine a 'setting' for the discussion of technics in the context of a 'work', or a body of work, such as Weber's? Doubtless the ambivalent processes of emplacement that place technics finally beyond absolute categorization, and which in turn open to questioning a variety of disciplinary boundaries and demarcations, tend to upset and disorient a sense of 'place' so as to expose technics to a range of topics and problems drawn from aesthetics and philosophy, and perhaps elsewhere. But the example drawn from Weber's writing on television clearly indicates that the manifestation or, indeed, the *thinking* of technics does not, nor cannot, take place *without* place. Rather, it is what might be called (borrowing from Derrida) an 'obscure economy' of placing and displacing, setting and upsetting – an agonized 'goings-on' without hope of hard conceptual distinction or dialectical resolution – that would characterize the place of technics in relation to (the) medium, to form, or to (the) institution: all in different ways concerns of Weber's *work*, which might itself be taken more generally to partake of, or find itself productively exposed to, what might be termed the disemplacements determining technics. This notion that there might be a technics *of* Weber's work – albeit perhaps an 'other' technics of technics, of the sort that characterizes an alternative (of sorts) to 'the calculations of technical rationality' – may suggest a useful line of approach in considering the continual and recursive re-posing or re-placing of certain texts, ideas and thinkers (an always transformative bringing-before and setting-into-place) which has characterized the iterative and performative dimensions of his critical procedures over the years. Nevertheless, a clear implication arises from the example taken from 'Television: Set and Screen'. Just as Heidegger's work emerges as a place from which the question of place is put into play, so the technics of Weber's work raise the question of the orientation of his writings, or more precisely how to orient a sometimes seemingly disparate range of readings and remarks having to do with orientation itself.

Technics and Aesthetic Judgement

This brings us back to Weber's essay 'The Unraveling of Form', in which he returns to the problem of aesthetic judgement in Kant, a problem previously explored by Weber in 'Ambivalence: The Humanities and the Study of Literature', included in his earlier book *Institution and Interpretation*. For this problem involves in itself a question of orientation. In the *Critique of Judgement*, aesthetic judgements furnish a prime instance of concern for Kant's critique insofar as they will always, to an extent, resist conceptual interpretation, being apparently derived from the subjective senses, while yet inevitably appealing to the already legible domains of established sorts of cognition so as to lay claim, quite unavoidably, to a kind of general validity. What, then, is the legitimacy of the process or activity of aesthetic judgement? Tied to this problem, by extension, is the question of how to found a transcendental critique of judgement in relation to aesthetic judgement as its carefully selected 'privileged object' (UF, 16). The range or field of possibilities generated here by the interplay of the demands of certitude, on the one hand, and the tenacious yet productively complementary presence of doubt, on the other, to some extent recalls Weber's evocation of the rationality of the subject in general after Cartesianism, where we find 'the calculations of a subjective will struggling to realize its representations and thereby to place itself in security' (US, 73). In a move that is also decisive for Weber's discussion of the institution of the humanities, he shows how Kant links aesthetic judgement to a notion of reflective judgement. Here, judgement is unable satisfactorily to determine individual phenomena simply by treating them as a case or example that can readily be subsumed under a more general category, rule or concept. Instead, in the absence of a fully determining law, principle or idea that might accord objectivity to the object or process at hand, Kant writes that reflective judgement treats unknown phenomena 'in accordance with such a unity as they would have if an understanding (although not our understanding) had furnished them to our cognitive faculties so as to make possible a system of experience according to particular laws of nature' (cited in UF, 18).[1]

Here, reflective judgement involves itself in a complex procedure in that, in order to arrive at its judgements, it must project and understand nature as purposive; and yet, in regarding nature as the product of an 'understanding', reflective judgement must view this 'understanding' as different from, outside or beyond its own, since its own 'understanding' is precisely incapable of bringing the phenomena at hand to satisfactory judgement. Aesthetic judgement is not, therefore, determined by its straightforward directedness or orientation in relation to an object. Instead, 'it must be directed at and determined by a singular other [that is, this 'other understanding'] that nonetheless possesses universality' (UF, 19). Weber writes that the 'name that Kant assigns to that other, which is neither the object nor the purely subjective hallucination, is *form*' (UF, 19). 'Form' is therefore ultimately the name given to the disemplacement, or the ambivalent process of unsecuring and securing, that happens in the somewhat rerouted or reoriented encounter of judgement, in its aesthetic or reflective guise, with the 'object' of its concern. For that matter, 'form' would also, by extension, effectively assign a name to a similar kind of process or movement which occurs in the encounter of transcendental critique with the problem of aesthetic judgement itself. This, more than just proposing an affinity between the movement and thinking of technics and the process and critique of judgement, suggests that the technics in and of deconstructive thinking of the kind pursued by Weber might also find their *place* in the portions of Kantian thought which, as we've seen Weber argue elsewhere, play such a crucial role in the thinking and founding of modern aesthetics and indeed in the very *institution* of the humanities:

> Kant's critical philosophy therefore bequeaths to the modern discipline of literary studies ... a fateful and ambiguous legacy. Literary and aesthetic judgements are assigned a decisive position within all the cognitive activities, inasmuch as such evaluations appear to be the exemplary instances of the judgemental process as such .... And yet at the same time aesthetic judgements provide no 'knowledge of its objects' and hence they cannot themselves be made the content of any substantive theory or discipline .... In short, the very dignity and significance of the aesthetic judgement as one in which the singularity of the object resists all attempts to subsume it under general concepts also precludes the establishment of a discipline of literary studies or of literary criticism. (A, 141)

The study of literature – as an exemplary figure of humanistic knowledge and inquiry – emplaces or institutes itself on the grounds of 'the ambiguous legacy' of 'Kant's critical philosophy', so that we find it takes *place*, as a discipline, just where *there are no safe places*. In other words, it secures its (institutional) place on the very basis of this 'unsecuring'. Once more, a technics is obviously detectable here.

Form, as the figure which establishes the ground or place of literary and, by extension, humanistic study, is, then, never safely or securely placed. Even though form serves to connect 'a multiplicity of sensations' (UF, 19) to produce some sort of perceptual unity, the very singularity demanded or presupposed by the object and process of aesthetic judgement entails a temporal and spatial specificity which, if form is reproduced or represented to serve the purposes of cognition or conceptualization, means that form itself must incessantly be in the process of transforming or deforming itself to survive. Thus, the '*delineating contour*' that seems to establish the very 'essence of form' necessarily begins to unravel in a process of 'undoing' that is, in fact, 'prescribed by the *aconceptual and singular universality* that, according to Kant, defines aesthetic judgement' (UF, 20).

Parergon and Institution

Weber tells us that the problem of aesthetic form in Kant is precisely what leads Derrida, in 'Restitutions', to the question of the parergon. If the fundamental purpose of form is to delineate and thereby demarcate the object, the contour or the frame in fact becomes 'the enabling limit of the work' (UF, 22): that which permits it to *take place*. However, even though it is the requisite condition of the work itself, Kant wants to distinguish the frame as not essential or proper to the aesthetic object, so as to avoid diminishing or even confounding the high status and standing of the latter. Yet Kant's decision to distinguish 'frame' from 'form' only *displaces* and *re-places* (recalling the figure of disemplacement) the dilemma it seeks to overcome. How can form be taken as a basis or standpoint from which to judge the aesthetic value or relevance of the frame, when it is the frame itself that determines form in the *first place*? Nevertheless, the frame must continue to be distinguished from the 'form' (for example, as having a certain non-aesthetic, functional or material quality) in order to determine, delimit or demarcate the work of art. Aesthetic thought and judgement must restrict, in the full sense, the notion that the frame, as an indispensable element in the composition of 'form', partakes of, or participates in, the aesthetic quality of the work, or else, as Weber puts it, 'just this participation would require another frame, an outer edge, in order for it to be determined as form' (UF, 23). Precisely because this constraining of the function or notion of the frame can only ever be partial (as, once more, a figure of the problematics of emplacement), the *place taken* by the frame remains profoundly uncertain as the encounter between 'form' or 'object' and aesthetic judgement itself *takes place*.

The question of the parergon, of form, work and frame, clearly raises the issue of institution in a variety of senses. At the most simple and obvious level, questions of the determination, demarcation or delimitation of something at least minimally recognizable as 'form' inevitably involve thinking about the process of *instituting*, although of course when thinking at this most obvious level it is important to remember that such instituting must thereby happen alongside – on condition of – the ongoing and dynamic operations, the rather agonized or conflictual *'goings-on'*, that, for Weber, always take place in the taking place of form. In addition, form and the parergon open on to questions of institution in that there is an evident correlation between the thinking concerning aesthetics and judgement going on in the portion of Kant's critical philosophy looked at so far, and the establishment of modern academic disciplines, especially in the humanities, which, Weber tells us, in fact 'owe much of their institutional legitimacy to the post-Kantian notion of a relatively autonomous "field" of enquiry' (UF, 24). In other words, Kantian problems of form and aesthetic judgement on which modern literary and humanistic study are – albeit shakily – founded also partake of the kinds of concern that enter into a thinking, after the Enlightenment, of the autonomy of a discipline or ' "field" of enquiry'. The extent to which the instituting of a 'coherent, integral, and self-contained domain' (LP, 26) in the field of knowledge depends on processes of differentiation that are inevitably conflictual and ambivalent is very carefully analysed by Weber in *Institution and Interpretation*, of course; and he continues to argue, in *Mass Mediauras*, that 'what is therefore at stake in these discussions is also ... the future of the university' (UF, 24). Between the discussion of technics in Heidegger and the revisiting of the problem of aesthetics and form in Kant, Weber is involved in a movement in which the question of institution is powerfully reinscribed. And, as is hopefully becoming apparent, this movement happens not just on the basis of a series of loosely-worked analogies. Rather, *institution* – as both a question in its own right and as the name for a critical procedure which constantly forms and de-forms (disorganizes) a set of readings, writings or interpretations that we might call Weber's 'work' – occupies a persistent yet never entirely stable place among Weber's other concerns (with technics, with aesthetics and so on) in a way that reactivates not just the themes but the very 'goings-on' of emplacement. It is this that permits us to speak of a technics *of* Weber. To formulate this a little further (even if the term or motif of formulation carries a certain irony here), one might also say that the technics *of* Weber partake of, or *assume*, the ambivalent processes of institution. If assuming the effects of ambivalence begins to transform knowledge into spectacle or, in effect, theatre, then it is in this vein that Weber's work *mimes* or *mimics* the work of technics and institution. It takes place just where there are no safe places. It secures its (institutional) place on the very basis of a persistent 'unsecuring'.

Institution, Technics and Theatre

The '*aconceptual and singular universality*' that emerges from the relation of aesthetic judgement to form in Kant causes the delineating contour or outline to begin to unravel into a 'scrawl'. As Kant's notion of form comes to be 'haunted by the shadowy tangle of inextricable traits' (UF, 25–26) that must accompany the singular qualities upon which he insists, Weber tells us: 'We are not very far here from those unlaced shoelaces that will so occupy Derrida in his discussion of Van Gogh's painting of shoes in "Restitutions" ' (UF, 26). This turns out to be a somewhat complex thread that Weber chooses not to pursue or pull on, although he would be 'authorized' to do so by the passage in Derrida's essay 'Mochlos', that connects Derrida's reflections on Heidegger's treatment of Van Gogh's painting of shoes in 'The Origin of the Work of Art' (and the subsequent rebuttal of Heidegger by Meyer Schapiro) to the reading in 'Mochlos' of Kant's *The Conflict of the Faculties*. Accordingly, the rethinking of aesthetics in Heidegger's 'Origin' – to which Weber soon returns in this essay on 'The Unraveling of Form' – is tied by Derrida not just to problems in Kant of, say, aesthetic judgement and form, but also, tellingly, to a text by Kant which contributes strongly to the founding of the modern university after the Enlightenment. To step back a little, perhaps, let us recall that, in 'Mochlos', Derrida writes:

> ... as Kant will have told us, the university will have to go on two feet, left and right, each foot having to support the other as it rises with each step to make the leap. It involves walking on two feet, two feet with shoes, since it turns on an institution, on a society and a culture, not just on nature. This was already clear in what I recalled about the faculty parliament. But I find its confirmation in an entirely different context, and you will certainly want to forgive me this rather rapid and brutal leap; I am authorized by the memory of a discussion, held in this very place some two years ago with our eminent colleague, Professor Meyer Schapiro, on the subject of certain shoes in Van Gogh. (M, 31–32)

As we've already seen, in his reading of *The Conflict of the Faculties* Derrida suggests that, just as the founding of the law cannot be viewed as simply a juridical question or decision, one either of legality or illegality, so the founding of the university cannot be treated as merely a 'university event' (M, 29). Rather, the founding of the university – akin to an act of performative force – must be considered as opening on to some 'other' from which it is received and which everywhere permeates it. Institution, like the imposition of form, takes place on *condition* of the other (which therefore, to some extent, *displaces* on the very occasion of *taking place*). Thus, the idea of the university as a unified and autonomously self-grounding institution with all its features based on the ideals or foundations of reason in fact founders, and the university is beset by a conflict which 'is interminable and therefore insoluble' (M, 28). There are no safe places where institution, as a species of technics (if one may say so), takes place. Such a conflict, taking place on condition of the other (and on condition of the taking place of technics), is therefore one that is itself difficult to *place*: as we have said, it can neither be attributed simply to an 'internal', 'logical' inconsistency or contradiction – an avoidable glitch in the university's design arising as an oversight, for example – nor easily dismissed as the result of 'outside' interference or intervention from government or society. A continuous crisis of legitimation thus ensues from a situation in which, as Derrida puts it, 'there can be no pure concept of the university ... due very simply to the fact that the university is *founded*'

(M, 29–30). This aporetical state of affairs gives rise to the problem of the university's orientation – a question of how it *finds* and *foots* itself, as much as one of its *founding*.

For Derrida, let us recall, Kant tries to reduce or forestall the intractable and destabilizing effects of this 'interminable crisis' by recasting the *conflict* of the faculties in place of the violently uncontainable forces one might associate with warfare (M, 28–29). The 'parliamentary solution' proposed by Kant 'internally' divides the university into higher and lower faculties occupying left and right benches, so as to orchestrate a closely regulated contest between those disciplines ultimately devoted to the conservation and defence of governmental statutes (that is, medicine, law and theology) and a more autonomous philosophical discipline serving the interests of 'truth'. Henceforth, the aporetical opening on to an inconceivable alterity is restaged in terms of a controlled structure or pattern of opposition (left versus right bench) which, in turn, ultimately gives rise to an overriding image of synthesis, unity and accord, via the inclusion or intervention of a transcendent third term – the parliamentary university itself. However, borrowing from Kant's 'What is Orientation in Thinking?' Derrida points out that right and left are, in fact, not to be construed in terms of 'conceptual or logical determination', but that they only acquire meaning and value in the region of 'a sensory topology that has to be referred to the subjective position of the human body' (M, 31). This means that, as 'directions', left and right cannot be objectively identified or secured from a universal or transcendent standpoint. The reduction of 'interminable crisis' to a 'parliamentary' opposition between the left and right benches or faculties therefore offers a no more reliable *standing* or *orientation* for the university, and indeed radically undermines the *position* Kant wants to secure for it – that is, that of a transcendent *standpoint* from which the conflict of the faculties might be both comprehended and resolved.

Disorientations between 'left' and 'right' of the kind explored in the previous chapter, both in relation to Derrida's reading of Kant in 'Mochlos' and Bahti's essay on 'The Injured University', convey an image of the university as a body suffering imbalance – a body unbalanced or off-balance. This would be a body, like that of the university, which is disoriented primarily because it is uncertain of its ground, and hence of its direction as well as of its foundation or institution, of its *emplacement* as much as of its *place*. While, in such a situation of imbalance, it is virtually impossible to know in advance how to proceed or, indeed, exactly what direction to take, the very image of this body 'off-balance' suggests not so much paralysis as continual movement of some kind, albeit of a body that is never entirely coordinated, a movement that is, finally, without determinable origin or end. Indeed, as has already been suggested, such movement indicates an (un-securing) play of kinetic energy which cannot be reduced or restricted to the more static designations associated either with a founding concept or idea, or a knowable 'object' or entity. Once again, then, we find ourselves in the realms of the problematics of technics. Drawing on Bahti's essay, let us recall that one may 'proceed' in this situation, if at all, only by means of a kind of leverage, which might itself occur by force of an ongoing 'imbalance' as the very condition of its possibility (IU, 73–74).

The imbalance and disorientation that propel the university from the *moment* of its institution derive from the agonized and ambivalent processes of institution itself. As we cannot avoid participating in them, it is these processes – taking place on condition or by *way* of an other – that begin to transform knowledge into spectacle or, in effect, theatre. In Kant's approach to the problem of aesthetic judgement as the exemplary object of a transcendental critique, unknown phenomena are treated, as we have seen, 'in accordance with such a unity as they would have if an understanding (although not our understanding) had furnished them to our cognitive faculties'. Here, via a certain reorientation or rerouting that seems to open up a dramaturgical space, knowledge takes place almost *as* a dramatization: it is staged, set and set up as spectacle – although in a sort of theatre which, in its essential yet ambivalent opening on to alterity, cannot fail to render more explicit the problem or issue of the bounding or the framing of its own space than is allowed by a contrary tug towards the determination of aesthetic 'form' or the 'work'.

Although Weber chooses not to pull on the thread that leads from Van Gogh's unlaced shoelaces via Derrida's 'Restitutions' and 'Mochlos' to Kant's *The Conflict of the Faculties*, the image of an institutional or instituted body propelled forward awkwardly or even comically is one that does crop up in another of Weber's discussions of institutional matters, as we've already seen. Here, such a body becomes overtly theatrical.

From the perspective of his reading of Kant, Weber argues that humanistic knowledge of the kind derived from literary study or aesthetic judgement originates in the question of thinking the 'singular'. In 'The Future of the Humanities: Experimenting', he relates the idea of singularity to a deconstructive thinking of iterability. Here, as with the *taking place* of form in Kant's *Critique of Judgement*, cognition or representation involves a repetition which nevertheless always alters or transforms. The 'singular' does not, therefore, name the uniqueness or integrity 'once-and-for-all' of a presence or being. Instead, the 'singular' is that which remains or persists after the taking place of an iterative process that *in fact* allows cognition and knowledge to take place. Though not without place, the 'singular' is, one may say, excessive and unplaceable. It is tenaciously resistant to the ordinary spatial and temporal determinations that might otherwise accord a unified presence 'in-itself'. It is for this reason that Weber describes the challenge to the humanities in terms of:

> ... *re-thinking the singular*, which is something very different from subsuming the individual under the general or the particular under the whole. The *singular* is not the *individual*, precisely by virtue of its mode of being, which can never be *simply* that of a once-and-for-all but rather, paradoxically, that of an aftereffect of iterability. The singular is that which is left over after the process of iteration has come full circle: it is the remnant or remainder. (FH, 245).

Such a thinking of iterability, which presents itself as an unavoidable provocation to the humanities, is linked by Weber to the question of repetition in and for philosophy, not least, as we've said, in regard to Kierkergaard's experimentation with certain lines of Kantianism. This experimentation, let us recall, involves the effort to articulate singularities 'without entirely dissolving ... differences into the similitude of the universal' (FH, 249). The always alterable-iterable 'actualities' which result from such experimenting suggest a performative style which gives rise to the question of theatre. However, the theatricality of the Kierkegaardian experiment disorganizes, traverses and exceeds the structure and effects associated with Aristotelian traditions of dramatic narrative, coming closer to *posse* theatre and acting, specifically the theatrical performances of an actor such as Beckmann, whose 'genius' is epitomized by, as Weber puts it, 'the way he enters the scene' (FH, 250). This entails an expression of possibility which, while it certainly seems to convey a sense of the 'actual' and 'immediate', nevertheless remains irreducible to a metaphysics of presence or to concomitant notions of self-identical 'objects' (of cognition) or (intentional) 'acts'. Hence, Weber draws attention to the remark of Constantin, Kierkegaard's 'pseudonymic author':

> In an art theater proper, one rarely sees an actor who can really walk and stand. As a matter of fact, I have seen only one, but what B. is able to do, I have not seen before. He is not only able to walk, but he is also able to *come walking*. To come walking is something very distinctive, and by means of this genius he also improvises the whole scenic setting. (Cited in FH, 251).[2]

If the humanities remain pervaded by the questions or problems one might associate with 'technics', so that it cannot plausibly present itself as a forum for producing stable 'objects' or self-identical phenomena (a 'standing stock') which might be taken to surpass spatio-temporal contingencies so as to lay the foundations for 'total' or universal claims within the domain of knowledge, then for Weber the humanities' future must be rethought in terms of a theatre of the singular, or, to be more precise, in terms of the *theatricality* of *singularities*. That is, such a future must be reimagined in light of a certain kind of theatricality, whereby the singular would repeat itself along the lines of Beckmann's very 'distinctive' or singular style of walking (as neverthless an unavoidably repetitive act) or, rather, along the lines of Constantin's rendition of it as that which (disjointing or disorganizing the space and time of Presence) *already is to come.*

Since, in Derrida's 'Mochlos', the founding of the university is not reducible to a mere 'university event', institution itself involves a relationship to alterity that is ultimately as uncertain as it is unstable, so that, likewise, the moment or *movement* by which the university founds, finds or foots itself cannot be tracked (tracked down, tracked back) in terms of a self-same point of origin or a 'first step'. Yet, instead of reaching or projecting ever backward to the always ungraspable horizon of such a point of origin that might be located in the past, the movement of institution which is thereby necessitated or entailed tends (if I can continue to risk the language of direction) to suggest an image or idea of propulsion forwards or onwards (although not in a crudely linear sense, a movement *somewhere* at least) via a proliferation of pluralizing singularities whose destination is nevertheless shifted or remapped each time of asking (in other words, a movement of leverage, a futural movement). The university not only 'walks on two feet', whereby a movement, a dis-placement, or a step depends on the leverage (or the footing or 'securing') received from the other (leg). Like Beckmann, the university 'comes walking'. Thus, the question of the university's *institution* is joined both to the play of technics, to the interminable process of 'securing' and 'unsecuring' that happens just where the movement of technics takes place, and to the effects of ambivalence that, in a strongly comedic performance of mimicry, turn or reduce knowledge to theatre. The turning or reduction of knowledge to theatre becomes all the more telling and, indeed, ironic when we recall that, as Weber reminds us, Heidegger always associated *techne* with *episteme* – with knowledge – but with a certain kind of knowledge whereby, as Heidegger writes:

> ... man, in midst of beings (*physis*) to which he is exposed (*ausgesetzt*), seeks to gain a stand (*einen Stand zu gewinnen*) and to establish himself, when in the process of mastering beings he proceeds in such and such a way, then this proceeding against beings is supported and guided by a knowledge of beings. This *knowledge* is called *techne*. (Cited in US, 59–60)[3]

Such a knowledge associated with technics should support man in the 'midst of beings', enabling him to 'gain a stand' and to 'establish himself' masterfully. Any such firm footing becomes much less sure, though, as we proceed or find our way (however disorientingly) from the play of technics, via the problems of form and institution, to the dramatization of knowledge, in which the orientation of man in the 'midst of beings' involves a movement that begins to look spectacularly comedic.

Technics, institution, theatre: the 'whole scenic setting' is improvised so that, with an uncontrollable burst of laughter, we are exposed to a series of 'goings-on' which, if they do not properly begin or found themselves, neither – like the 'goings-on' of modern technology – can they can stop.

Odradek

Weber concludes his essay on 'The Unraveling of Form' with a reading of Kafka's short story, 'The Cares of a Family Man', which he otherwise translates as 'The Concerns of a House Father'. Here, we are confronted with Odradek. This unusual word 'catches our attention' at the beginning of the tale. It is of 'uncertain origin' and remains 'enigmatic' in meaning 'despite the most persistent etymological efforts' (UF, 31). However, as the word reveals itself to be a name or noun, a description of the thing itself takes the place of an etymological investigation of meaning. Yet the object or 'thing' designated by this term turns out to be just about as 'enigmatic' as the word which names it. On first inspection, Odradek looks like a flat star-like spool, covered with, as Weber puts it:

> ... worn-out bits and pieces of thread, tangled up and twisted.... The threads are thus neither discrete threads, nor something entirely different from thread. They are threads in the process of becoming threadbare.... This tangle of traits makes the figure extremely difficult to delineate. (UF, 32)

What is tangled up in the contemplation of this object or 'thing' is, most obviously, the unravelling of form itself. Odradek as both (un)translatable word and 'enigmatic' thing takes place amid 'an inextricably convoluted tangle of traits' (UF, 27) which is always in the process of ravelling and unravelling. Insofar as it constitutes any sort of form at all, Odradek nonetheless 'never quite gets its act sufficiently together' (UF, 27) (and here I begin to borrow or displace phrases that Weber deploys elsewhere in his essay) to form an entirely recognizable object. Thus, Odradek is nothing other than the 'repository of the trait that is no longer defined as the outer edge' (UF, 27). Odradek is made up of a tangle of traits, and these traits proliferate, pervade and constitute Odradek as a thing (and, indeed, as a name), rather than establishing a single, unifying trait tracing a contour or outline along the 'outer edge', which in more traditional aesthetics delineates 'form' by means of 'frame'. (It is worth pointing out here that Weber's discussion of Odradek rests upon Heidegger's notion, in 'The Origin of the Work of Art', of the *Riß* – a more or less untranslatable term nevertheless translated as rift/design – as that which draws or 'tears' together the conflicting forces that dynamically structure the work.) Nevertheless, this continual unravelling of 'form' and 'frame' does not stop Odradek from taking place. The lack of clarity or recognizability that surrounds Odradek in the etymological, conceptual and visual or cognitive realms render it exceptionally fluid on a variety of levels. But even if it is therefore, in Kafka's tale, 'always on the move', 'extraordinarily mobile' and 'impossible to catch' (cited in UF, 33),[4] Odradek must continue literally to take its place, to re-place itself, as indeed 'the mode in which it *is*' (UF, 27). Like Heidegger's work of art, then, Odradek is thereby structured or tangled together by a conflictual play of forces – for example, those which simultaneously 'secure' and 'unsecure' its place. For all its impenetrable mystery, Odradek is never *without* place, but on the contrary must continue to secure a place for itself. Engaging with Kafka's text, Weber writes:

> By means of one of the crossbars and the point of its star 'the whole can stand upright, as though on two legs'. Anything that can 'stand' or be stood upright, 'as though on two legs', obviously can lay claim to a more complex mode of being than that of a mere spool of thread. (UF, 32)

This taking of a stand on Odradek's part somewhat comically mimes the attempt of man to 'gain a stand' in the 'midst of beings' by drawing on the support offered by the knowledge associated with technics. By standing in a relation of mimicry to 'man' in the context of a 'whole scenic setting' which suggests, again, the complexly interwoven traits that entangle technics, form, theatre and institution, Odradek no doubt acquires a more complex mode of being. Indeed, since Kafka's text suggests that 'this assemblage' tempts us to believe it once had 'some sort of purposive form', Weber writes: 'We have before us, in short, the perfect Kantian aesthetic object: purposive form without purpose, structure without meaning' (UF, 32). Perfect Kantian aesthetic object Odradek may be. Yet, at the same time, it remains tangled up with the unravelling of form and the play of technics that impels and propels the 'goings-on' of institution (those of the institution of the humanities, for example), and which compels the university, in the comic, theatricalized style of Beckmann, to 'come walking' – on two undecidably left and/or right feet.

Taking its always uncertain place amid the play of technics, the unravelling of form, the founding and footing of institution, and the event or advent of theatre, is Odradek synonymous with the work of Samuel Weber?

Notes

1   This quote is taken from the Introduction to Kant's *Kritik der Urteilskraft* (Darmstadt: Wissenschaftliche Buchgesellschaft, 1983), § IV, 180. The translation is Weber's.
2   The reference here is to Kierkegaard's *Fear and Trembling/Repetition*, ed. and trans. Howard V. Hong and Edna H. Hong (Princeton, NJ: Princeton University Press, 1983), 163.
3   This quote is taken from Martin Heidegger, *Nietzsche*, Bd. I (Pfullingen: Gunther Neske, 1961). The translation is Weber's.
4   Here, and throughout the last section of 'The Unraveling of Form', Weber quotes from Franz Kafka, 'Die Sorge eines Hausvaters', in *Samtliche Erzahlungen* (Frankfurt am Main: Fischer, 1981), 157. The translation is his own.

Chapter 4

Theatricality

The Kantian problem of aesthetic form, such as is treated by Derrida in *The Truth in Painting*, remains decisive for Weber, as we've seen, in unravelling the relations of form, technics, institutions, and theatre. The delineation and hence the demarcation of an object, upon which the very conception of aesthetic form depends, requires the contour or frame (of the 'work', for example) to be clearly distinguished, and to remain distinguishable. Henceforth, however, the frame itself appears to have a constitutive function, serving as 'the enabling limit of the work'. Kant, of course, wishes to downplay the importance of the frame as neither proper nor essential to the form of the aesthetic object. Yet in attempting to distinguish between 'frame' and 'form' so as to be able to take the latter as a standpoint or basis from which to judge – and from which to dismiss – the aesthetic value or pertinence of the frame, Kant alludes to an *a priori* conception of form, the legitimacy of which remains in question since its *form* as a concept cannot yet have been properly *delineated*, preceding, as it does, the supposedly secondary term of the 'limit', border or frame. The 'frame' must therefore remain an indispensable element in the composition of 'form' and thus cannot be distinguished or excluded so decisively in relation to the formal properties of the aesthetic object. The very concept of form, and, indeed, the very form of the concept, cannot be exempted from that which would appear to set it apart. Yet the fact that the 'limit' or 'edge' of the work irreducibly partakes of, and participates in, the 'form' which it would otherwise serve to particularize means that, as Weber tells us, 'just this participation would require another frame' (UF, 23) for the aesthetic object to be comprehended *as such*. And then, presumably, as this frame once more partakes of its constitutive function as an indispensable element in the composition of form, *another*. And then *another* ....

The limits of aesthetic form, and indeed of the aesthetic judgement which is called for in this portion of Kant's critical philosophy, must henceforth be construed rather differently. The conception of the frame as an outer edge or margin, a continuous perimeter or unbroken contour, now gives way to the problem of the parergon, in which the 'limit' unstably and unavoidably proliferates, traverses and dislocates (itself) in the very *taking place*, the very division or setting apart, of the aesthetic object or form. The limit continually divides and redivides (itself). Such unstable and ongoing processes of division do not merely indicate the always provisional and precarious nature of the borders of the aesthetic object; more fundamentally, they would seem to 'internally' divide *ad infinitum* our very notions of 'inner' and 'outer', putting into perpetual deconstruction the conceptual opposition of the two. Indeed, one effect of such far-reaching deconstructibility is, obviously, that it becomes much less satisfactory to speak merely of an 'internal' division which might be found in our conception of what is 'inside' or what is 'outside' aesthetic limits, as if the problem could be reduced to a matter of logical contradiction or dialectical interplay. Rather, (the problem of) aesthetic form and judgement is subject to the dislocating force of an alterity not reducible to those categorizations of otherness which continue to operate on the basis of some more sustainable, more workable distinction – or even interplay – between 'outside' and 'inside'.

Such problems prove enormously productive as they find their way into Weber's writings on a number of different occasions, and in view of a variety of topics. We have already seen how the question of the parergon is crucial for Weber's thinking regarding the question of technics. Via Weber's discussion of 'emplacement' as a movement which both opens up and closes down, secures and unsecures, places and displaces, locates and dislocates, the impossibility of determining 'technics' as simply a question *either* for 'the sciences' *or* 'the arts' becomes evident; and indeed, rather than simply being suspended or dispensed with here, the question of the borderline and interplay between the two continues to remain a tenacious and complex issue. It should come as no surprise, then, that the problem of determining 'form' which arises both in the vicinity of aesthetic judgement and technical knowledge is never far from Weber's wide-ranging reflections upon the conflictual aspects of the processes of institution. And since institution and interpretation remain indissolubly linked for Weber – in the sense that the institution (of literary criticism, of the humanities, or indeed of psychoanalysis) arises only *on condition* of interpretive conflict – the parergon is called to mind throughout Weber's analysis of the struggle to establish a comprehensive theory of 'aesthetic response': the term Wolfgang Iser adopts as a label for his theory of reading. Here, as Weber is able to demonstrate, theoretical description cannot avoid the activity of reading it seeks to describe, transcend or position securely as an 'object' of knowledge outside itself. Proving itself partial to that it would seek to particularize or set apart (that is, reading), the 'theoretical' effort that remains indispensable to the processes of founding, consolidating or reorienting the disciplinary space of literary study exemplifies the *particular* and non-totalizable character of the institution's 'systematicity'. In other words, the institution is ultimately unable either to fully incorporate or absolutely exclude those forces at play in its own institutionalization. Instead, since a comprehensive theoretical description of reading as an 'object' of knowledge, such as is attempted by Iser, must entail resorting to somewhat partial and partisan practices of reading in order to found itself, the general system or framework uncannily (re)doubles itself in the *particular* it wishes to transcend or surpass. Once more, far from simply drawing the line, the 'limit' redivides (itself), doubles, dislocates. It doubles and dislocates not just the 'internal' space of that which it is supposed to demarcate. Its effects don't just stop there. For in doubling, dislocating and continually redividing the very limit that is supposed to separate or hold apart such a space from the 'outside', the parergon exposes us to a more radical alterity. Here, the coming of the 'other' is not just the coming of an outsider.

It may appear, therefore, that the problem of the parergon or limit is put to *unlimited* use in Weber's work, spanning his discussions of institutions, interpretation, disciplinarity, technics, psychoanalysis, deconstruction and, as we shall see, theatricality. And yet, paradoxically enough, if the limit was indeed simply unlimited here, it would hardly be possible even to begin distinguishing, describing or particularizing such a 'work'. Nevertheless, if we might wish to 'frame' in some wider way the 'work' of Samuel Weber by alluding or resorting to the problem of the parergon, this must obviously be considered quite inappropriate or *improper*: the parergon hardly offers the possibility of a simple framework, in view of which the characteristic features, orientation and bounds of a 'work' might decisively be comprehended and articulated. The parergon obviously calls us to radically question traditional conceptions of the 'work' itself. When addressing questions of the limit *in* Weber's 'work' and the limit *of* his 'work', of what distinguishes certain parts of his writing in relation to others, or indeed what characterizes his texts in general in regard to the work of others, the parergon therefore emerges as an indispensable yet improper 'framework' which subjects us to the thought and force of the 'other' *as* or *at* the very limit of such categories, distinctions or oppositions. And we must ask whether Weber's 'work' *assumes*, iterates or performs such limits and, if so, how?

Theatrical Limits

The parergon also offers an 'improper' framework for approaching the question of Weber's interest in theatricality. For what can be considered inside or outside theatre? What bounds the theatrical scene? How and where can we trace its edge? Describing the performative dimensions of deconstruction in the interview 'Goings On', a performativity which Weber associates with highly focused practices paying detailed attention to the singular and sometimes oblique or obscure aspects of an issue or a text, he points out that:

> ... 'performance' should ... not be understood to deny the 'reality' of power relationships that characterize the world in which we work and live. We have to make judgements, 'take' decisions, evaluate situations. But such efforts are not simply means to an end independent of them. They are caught up in what they seek to grasp, discern, transform; and that involvement can perhaps best be described in terms of the relation of 'performance' and 'play'. Does such a theatrical perspective take reality too lightly? Or, on the contrary, does it do justice to the complexity – and indeed, to the *ambivalence* – of our involvement in the world? (GO, 229–30)

If the performative quality of deconstructive practice often leads to deliberately playful readings and writings which seem to flout the protocols and propriety expected of academic scholarship – just because, as Weber notes in another discussion, 'Catching Up with the Past', 'it is not considered "serious" [for academics] to use language as anything other than an instrument for the communication of meaning' (CU, 179) – then, for Weber, it is far from a simple matter to distinguish this playfulness and theatricality from what might in fact be most 'serious', going beyond the confines of theatre – at least, as it is more narrowly conceived. Indeed, it is by way of a 'theatrical perspective' such as Weber associates with deconstructive writing and practice that the more wide-ranging experience or situation of being 'caught up' in what we seek to 'grasp, discern, transform' is reflected, replayed and redoubled. This situation of being 'caught up' is something that, as we've seen, Weber discerns in the attempt to establish a theory of reading or aesthetic response, and which he detects in the effort to found and defend an institution such as psychoanalysis. But it is also by means of this description of the theatrical situation as one of being 'caught up' that Weber allows himself to speak further of 'the complexity – and indeed ... the *ambivalence* – of our involvement in the world'. (Here, the limits of the analysis are obviously opened up, although the complex and specific dynamics of ambivalence that Weber frequently investigates arrest any simple movement towards totalization or universality in view of the question of theatricality.) Going further still, Weber suggests that it is by means of such a 'theatrical perspective' that the question or possibility arises of 'doing justice' – although to 'do' justice, not least insofar as deconstruction is concerned, remains a highly complex and perhaps unresolvable issue. At any rate, these remarks concerning the performative aspect of deconstruction suggest that theatricality, for Weber, names the experience or situation – the *performance* – of an unavoidable yet always partial and specific participation in that which we variously attempt to comprehend, describe, delimit, delineate, observe, identify, objectify, interpret or analyse. Here, then, the unstable processes of repetition and dislocation that occur on condition of the deconstructibility of 'frames' or frameworks give rise to scenarios which, for Weber, can be explored most interestingly in terms of 'theatricality'.

But let us ask again, even in view of a more narrow idea of the 'theatrical': what can be considered outside or inside theatre? What are its bounds? How and where can its limit be marked or its edge be traced? For example, is the theatrical boundary synonymous with the borders of the stage or can it be located instead at the outer limits of the audience? In light of the ambivalent relations or the conflictual dynamics of performance, participation, apartness and setting apart to which Weber continually draws our attention, is it possible to secure or stabilize either of these 'limits' quite so easily or, indeed, to uphold a distinction between the two? Furthermore, where are the limits of scene and play, when each 'frame' would seem inexorably to call for another? Stage, audience, scene, and play immediately suggest a number of spatial and temporal limits, but just *how* do these supply the frames or the framework for theatricality? How do they combine or contrast with one another, or indeed do they conflict with or dislocate (double, redivide) themselves and one another? As has been suggested a number of times already, theatricality is the term that we might associate with the kinds of question and effect that Weber wants to explore when the supposedly autonomous, coherent or self-contained structures or domains of 'form', 'work', 'theory', 'discipline', 'institution' and 'knowledge' are exposed to the constitutive yet dislocating force of the 'other'. But are the very *limits* of theatricality themselves subject to this alterity, which, since it is not reducible to the binary opposition or dialectical interplay of inside–outside, can no more be considered the 'inner' trait or essence of theatricality than it can be described as a sort of 'outsider' intruding upon the supposedly 'non-theatrical' domains listed above?

Taking Place, Dislocating Theatre

These introductory comments and questions, then, inevitably serve to frame a discussion of theatricality in Weber's writings, but they also continually work to exceed, destabilize and dislocate any framework in which the question of theatricality *as such* might be put. If the problem and the effects of theatricality cannot be reduced to detached theoretical description of the kind entailed in positing a coherent and self-contained concept or object of cognition and knowledge, then it remains to be seen how Weber's writing partakes of the kinds of theatricality he wishes to explore, and how this theatricality is at work in his own texts. To begin to approach this question, I want to turn to two essays by Weber, on opera and on psychoanalysis.

In 'Taking Place: Toward a Theater of Dislocation' Weber describes the Frankfurt Opera's staging of *Aida* in January 1981. Although heralded as signalling a 'decisive "breakthrough"' (TP, 108–109) for the Frankfurt Opera Company, the initial performances of *Aida* were met with 'intense indignation' by those sections of the audience committed to traditional operatic dramaturgy. In his essay, Weber pays particular attention to the opening scene – 'or, rather, the scene that preceded the opening of the drama, since it accompanied the overture' (TP, 107). Such a 'scene', upon which Weber wants to place a great deal of emphasis, therefore seems to usher in the 'work' itself. Yet, while this scene takes place at – or, indeed, *as* – the very threshold of the opera, it remains difficult to *place* in relation to the 'work' *proper*: does this scene stand inside or outside the 'work'? Does it 'precede' or 'open' the opera, or, somehow, do both? In this 'opening' scene, we find Ramades, captain of the Egyptian palace guard, 'dressed in the civilian clothes of a nineteenth-century European businessman' and 'in what appears to be a dream, he seizes a shovel (implausibly located in what appears to be an office) and begins to dig the earth, or, rather, to tear up the floorboards of the stage, bringing to light first sand, then a sword, and finally the sculpted head of Aida' (TP, 107). For Weber, Ramades – in a scene that seems bizarre enough to resemble a dream – acts to call into question the space in which theatrical representation takes place. Indeed, by digging into the very foundations of that space, Ramades 'opens' the opera with a gesture that is at once undeniably self-referential yet which, at the same time, precludes the scene's self-containment. If the violent and seemingly deranged shovelling of Ramades works profoundly to disturb, rather than to convey, the reassuring '"dreamy" quality' (TP, 120) a traditional audience might expect of Verdi's prelude, it is nevertheless precisely because this dream-scene dislocates the work as a self-contained structure (one thereby possessed of determinable, authoritative, univocal meaning) that it replaces, according to Weber, 'the traditional aesthetics of *Darstellung*' with 'a theater of *Entstellung*' (TP, 121).

Ramades' digging, then, undermines – by exposing and calling into question – the hitherto taken-for-granted foundations of dramatic representation. It disorganizes the 'traditional, self-contained' (TP, 117) space of theatre rather than just dismantling it (for in digging up the floorboards, Ramades nevertheless does not move outside the space of this dream-scene), and it does so, first and foremost, by drawing up and including in the scene the enabling limits or foundations of theatre. Far from remaining 'neutral', then, these 'limits' become 'an integral part of the show itself' (TP, 118). Weber is quick to point out that the foundations which thereby become an irreducible component of the performance are, above all, *material*. That materiality, he tells us, 'includes not merely the actual floorboards of the stage, but the entire social system upon which theater depends' (TP, 117). This social system is underpinned by a variety of attitudes, practices and institutions which, Weber tells us, can be characterized in terms of 'nostalgic idealization and identification', whereby the 'exotic – the distant, heroic, sumptuous Golden Age of the Bourgeoisie – is made familiar' (TP, 111). Such effects occur by way of an 'exercise in recognition', as Adorno puts it (cited in TP, 111).[1] Yet if 'exotic artificiality is built into operatic form' (TP, 116), and if it is very much expected by the more conservative operagoer, then, for Weber, an alienation effect along Brechtian lines will be insufficient to call into question traditional operatic dramaturgy. For, Weber asserts, 'if audiences identify with opera today, it is precisely because of its distance, not in spite of it' (TP, 116). To the extent that it is shocking, Ramades' violence, according to Weber, cannot simply be reduced to a strategy of *Verfremdung*, since what the conventional operagoer generally expects to be foregrounded and celebrated during the performance is a highly contrived and self-conscious theatricality, tied to the lavish rendition of a now-remote historical epoch. Since opera's 'exotic artificiality' is irreducibly linked to effects of identification and illusion which are promoted so as to secure the ideological disposition of the spectator, it remains questionable whether this 'exotic artificiality' should be distinguished quite so decisively in relation to the conventions of naturalistic drama.

According to Weber, of course, such a decisive distinction between operatic and naturalistic theatre is what forces us to rule out *Verfremdung* in the opera as a meaningful strategy or source of critique and resistance. Nevertheless, Weber is right to point out that, in one sense, Ramades' digging profoundly disorganizes the space and foundations of theatre often taken for granted by 'reactionary' and Marxist dramaturgy alike. He writes, 'as generally understood, the notion of *alienation* supposes precisely the traditional, Euclidean notions of space that stagings such as the one we are discussing seek to problematize: a space in which distance and proximity are mutually exclusive' (TP, 116–17). That is, when comparing the dramatic theory and practice of naturalism with the theatre of alienation, relationships of detachment and engagement are obviously configured very differently; yet in each case they are imagined to be subject to the controlled and calculated design, or intention, of a theatrical strategy which rests upon the conceptual coherence of the distinction between what is proximate and what is distant in spatial terms. In the opening scene of the Frankfurt Opera's *Aida*, however, 'something far more disquieting takes place, something which can no longer be understood in terms of the ultimately reassuring opposition of "outside" and "inside." What is represented onstage is an act that calls the space in which it "takes place" into question' (TP, 117). The spatial relationships and distinctions presupposed by a more traditional and secure conception of *place* are subjected to the maddening force of their own deconstructibility, since the import of those (material) foundations which Ramades puts (or folds) back into (the) play as an 'integral part' can be determined only by reference to the theatrical context which they had hitherto served to delimit, but which they now come to disorganize and dislocate.

In a similar vein, although the objects which Ramades brings up along with the floorboards of the stage – namely, the sword and the sculpture – are normally taken to embody the traditional and reassuring connotations of glory and art, power and love, this interpretation depends upon a taken-for-granted conception of the operatic 'work' and event, the *taking place* of which is now thrown into disarray just as the 'integral part' of the theatrical limit or foundation is exposed or revealed. Henceforth, the opera simply cannot be contained, simply cannot contain itself; and it is, in the widest possible sense, now 'no longer a suitable object of identification' (TP, 116). Indeed, this remains true even in view of the nineteenth-century costume and setting in which we find Ramades. This might seem to conjure up the 'Golden Age of the Bourgeoisie' and hence provide a 'suitable object of identification', yet, as Weber writes: 'Like the stage floor, the historical context of … emergence is inscribed in, or rather *as*, the scene that "ushers in" the work; once again the enabling limits of the opera are folded back into the spectacle itself' (TP, 121). Once more, then, this re-inclusion of the 'enabling limit' happens in a way that, for Weber, both opens up and dislocates the framework of theatrical representation.

If the opera is 'no longer a suitable object of identification', let us recall that such identification – providing the grounds for 'nostalgic idealization' – is, of course, an enabling feature of 'an entire social system' having its own material basis. Thus, where the material foundation of the opera becomes 'an integral part of the show itself', a better description of this theatrical 'limit' would be of a *dis-integral* part. For, Weber tells us, 'this part is one that calls the whole into question' (TP, 118): the authoritative intentionality of the 'work', the coherence and self-containment of the operatic event, and the (self-) recognition of the audience. Hence, if the framework according to which theatricality is conventionally understood itself breaks down or divides into a series of structuring partitions or 'frames' – the stage, the theatre, the audience, the scene, the play – then, far from combining harmoniously as self-consistent elements in order to allow the whole to come full circle, these 'frames' dislocate themselves and one another in the Frankfurt Opera's *Aida*:

Once the limits of the scene, the foundations of this site, are thus included in the scene itself, the space of representation can no longer simply be taken for granted or unequivocally delimited. Who is to say where it starts, and where it stops? The audience, finding itself on the spot and yet unable to determine where that spot is located, is put out: exasperated by a space in which it is not entirely at home, and yet which it knows all too well. The opera house has ceased to be a home. (TP, 118)

It is this, above all, that disorganizes the desire of the audience for (self-) recognition: for how can it hope to recognize what it cannot definitively locate? Once the limits of the scene are no longer neutral, the spectacle is no longer securely in place, nor are the spectators.

For some, Weber might be digging too deep in order to imbue Ramades' shovelling with a greater degree of importance than it deserves. For in order to confirm the value of a 'theatrical perspective' such as is offered or practised by deconstruction, whereby 'performance' and 'play' are seen as inseparable from the 'complexity' and 'ambivalence' of 'our involvement in the world', is it enough to celebrate the 'decisive "breakthrough"' of the Frankfurt Opera Company in unsettling the assumptions and expectations of the traditional operagoer? In Weber's own terms, 'Does such a theatrical perspective take reality too lightly?'. Despite Weber's remarks concerning the material basis of a specific social system and group for which opera is traditionally an important tool of self-recognition, does the operatic 'performance' and 'play' that he wishes to dwell upon here in fact lead us away from, rather than towards, 'involvement in the world'?

The attention paid by Weber in regard to the Frankfurt Opera's *Aida*, and to Ramades' digging in particular, calls to mind his own depiction of deconstructive reading and practice. The 'small detail' (if we may call it that) of this opening or preceding scene, which might be construed as of minor significance when compared to the grandeur and seriousness of the operatic 'work' *proper* (let alone in relation to important issues in the 'outside world'), is not merely taken to exceed its own, particular limits. Since it 'takes place' at the very *threshold* of the opera, such small detail calls into question the very limits that delimit aesthetic form, 'work', dramatic unity and, indeed, the identity of the audience. And, as these limits come to be 'included' so as to disorganize and dislocate the very forms and spaces which they are supposed to delineate and demarcate, it becomes all the more difficult to decide *how* and *where* to delimit aesthetics in regard to politics, representation in relation to reality, elitism as distinct from what might be termed the 'everyday'. As Weber puts it 'Who is to say where it starts, and where it stops?'. Just where Ramades digs, there is no longer a stable *basis* for assuming that the importance of this little 'scene' stops with the question of operatic

dramaturgy or, indeed, the particular cultural proclivities of a hugely
privileged social elite.

A Theatre of *Entstellung*

But what, then, is the wider importance of this little scene? And in what
ways does it help us return to the questions with which we began? If, in
regard to the opening scene of the Frankfurt Opera's *Aida*, one might
indeed ask 'Who is to say where it starts, and where it stops?', then
exactly how does Weber's writing itself partake of the kinds of
theatricality he wishes to explore? How is this theatricality at work in his
own texts, and with what effects? Perhaps most importantly, when
considering these effects, what is the extent of *their* significance?

When Weber tells us that 'what is represented onstage [when
Ramades digs] is an act that calls the space in which it "takes place"
into question', he is guilty of a rare lapse in precision. For Ramades'
deranged and violent shovelling dislocates and disorganizes the scene in
a way that allows Weber, elsewhere in his essay, to speak of a shift from
'the traditional aesthetics of *Darstellung*' to 'a theater of *Entstellung*' –
one of distortion, disfigurement and dislocation. It is therefore
inappropriate to speak of Ramades' gesture in terms of an *act* – and
here the implication is of a deliberate 'political' strategy and rationale at
work in the opening sequence of the opera – not just because it takes
place during something like a dream-scene, in which conscious ideas and
decisions are all but confounded by unconscious processes and drives.
More importantly, if the disorganizing and dislocating force of
Ramades' digging ushers in not the 'work' but instead a theatre of
Entstellung, then we should never expect to excavate an original
intention that organizes the meaning (or the indeed, the narrative) one
might elaborate in terms of the scene's significance. For his violence to
be considered an *act* in the sense of prosecuting an explicit and
deliberate 'political' intention, decision or strategy, surely Ramades
would need to attain a degree of exteriority, however minimal, in
relation to the 'dream'? He would surely need, in some sense, to move or
operate voluntarily, 'outside' the dream-scene, especially one that ushers
in a theatre of *Entstellung*. Yet not only does Ramades *not* move outside
this theatrical space; his digging serves to disorganize the 'reassuring
opposition of "outside" and "inside"' which would seem to provide the
basis and orientation for a traditional conception of the voluntary or
volitional (political) act. This also means that the audience, while they
are undeniably 'put out' by his highly contentious and shocking gesture,
can no more act independently of it (for it is the dislocating part of a
'scene' that defies identification and re-cognition) than Ramades can
intervene to control or determine its meaning by adopting the

standpoint of an intentional agent. The dream's structure as *Entstellung* therefore provides something like 'an allegory of the Freudian unconscious', as Weber, in a footnote to the essay, puts it. Here, 'the position of the spectator is revealed as both specious and unavoidable' (*OE*, 252–53). It is unavoidable, in the sense that the spectator unavoidably *dreams* the dream of Ramades: the audience is exasperated, somehow put on the spot or, rather, put out, but bewilderingly they seem unable to act, or to escape, in relation to that which they cannot definitively recognize or locate. The operagoer *as* dreamer, then, 'appears to be a mere observer of the dream', yet this turns out to be 'merely part of the dream's structure as *Entstellung*' (*OE*, 253), in which the audience cannot help but be included, so that the spectatorial standpoint is at the same time 'specious'. As Weber therefore tells us of the dream's structure as *Entstellung*, the perspective of the spectator is 'ineluctable' but nevertheless 'remains inscribed in a spectacle that no glance can oversee' (*OE*, 253). As one particular theatrical limit or 'frame' – one structuring partition of the general framework that gives us our traditional conception of theatre – the audience here do not merely trace out the 'edge' of the drama in terms of a spectatorial vantage-point from which the 'work' can be definitively comprehended, or the opera appraised. Instead, since this very same liminality turns out to be 'specious', 'merely part of the dream's structure as *Entstellung*', the audience are also drawn into the theatrical (and theatricalized) space precisely by means of the specious impression of mere spectatordom. But does 'just this participation ... require another frame', and *another*, and *another* ... as the characteristic or condition of a 'spectacle that no glance can oversee'? Is this the theatre's, or the dream's, structure as *Entstellung*? And, if so, how might the 'structure' of *Entstellung* also describe (although not in the sense of marking out or drawing a line around) the scene or the staging of Weber's own writings, taking his speculations concerning a variety of phenomena, issues and texts 'beyond' mere spectatorship of the kind associated with more traditional conceptions and renditions of knowledge?

Weber's essay 'The Blindness of the Seeing Eye' offers a succinct yet illuminating discussion of *Entstellung* in Freud's writing. As has been indicated, this term signifies distortion, but, according to Weber, carries the sense of dislocation as much as of disfigurement in Freud. For Freud, dreams cannot be considered *in terms of their latent content* ultimately to harbour a single, determinable meaning, nor, therefore, are they reducible to a self-contained object of cognition that is susceptible to 'a hermeneutics that defines its task in terms of *explication* or of *disclosure*' (BS, 79). Instead, dreams constitute themselves, as Weber puts it, 'through, and as, interpretation' (BS, 77), which must itself be conceived in terms of a process that is closer to *Entstellung* than *Darstellung* (the latter signifying presentation or exposition). Freud tells us that the dream manifests 'a particular *form* of thinking' (cited in BS, 79)[2] which Weber describes as 'that of a de-formation which serves to dissimulate its deformative character by creating a representational façade' (BS, 79). While Freud insists that all dreams are in principle liable to interpretation (although not general theoretical categorization or reduction as such) the dream's dissimulation should therefore not be construed as a veil to be penetrated by the interpretive effort of a traditional hermeneutics, in order to reveal a fully determinable object, the ultimate meaning of the dream *itself*. Instead, the 'representational façade' dissimulates the 'essence' of the dream-work as a form of 'thinking', interpretation, distortion or dislocation occurring as the effect of conflictual wish-fulfilment. In *The Interpretation of Dreams*, Freud therefore writes: 'It is true that we distort dreams in attempting to reproduce them ... but this distortion (*Entstellung*) is itself no more than a part of the elaboration which the dream-thoughts regularly undergo as a result of the dream-censorship' (cited in BS, 78).[3] The interpretation of dreams is thus a dislocating repetition and a repetitious dislocation of the dream: it should be construed in terms of *Entstellung* as discerned by Freud in the dream-work, arising on condition of a conflictual wish-fulfilment which cannot be set apart as simply a characteristic feature of dreaming when asleep, for example. (Indeed, in 'The Meaning of the Thallus', one of the subsections of *The Legend of Freud*, Weber takes Freud's insight further, and writes: 'The logic of identity takes its place in the dream's strategy of displacement as that which dissimulates the distortions that have taken place, have taken *the* place of the conscious mind precisely by seeming to yield to it' (*LF*, 103).)

Returning to *Aida*, if the interpretive effort of the audience founders when 'confronted' with the dream-scene in which Ramades disorganizes the foundations of stage (and, thereby, those of dramatic representation), it is because, far from shedding light upon an original intention, a fundamental meaning, and hence a separable object of cognition, Ramades' digging entails a kind of 'dream-work' that ushers in a theatre of *Entstellung* in which all must participate and which none can simply oversee. And if 'just this participation ... require[s] another frame' in order for such a theatre of *Entstellung* to be recognized or distinguished at all, then nevertheless the interpretive effort of the critic – Weber himself – can no more be divorced from the effects of dislocating repetition or repetitious dislocation that it wishes (and yet does not wish) to 'describe'. For these effects are not only pervasive, but always already at play.

How, then, might we read Weber's texts so as to discern an alternative to the long-standing model of interpretation, predicated upon '*explication*' or '*disclosure*', that is associated with traditional hermeneutics; an alternative which cannot merely be proposed, but which must be *assumed* as already at work or at play in his writing (on theatricality, for instance, the limits of which are far from certain)? Such an alternative interpretive practice would necessarily be less recognizable in terms of conventional academic scholarship, although perhaps (like Ramades) it might serve to *re-place* it, less in the sense of seeking to dismantle or move outside its space, than by serving to disorganize and call into question the assumptions and distinctions that would otherwise serve to distinguish and demarcate such 'scholarship' from charlatanism, amateurism, intellectual imposture and so forth. On the basis of the previous discussion, this 'alternative', as bizarre as it might sound, would therefore be more closely allied to *dreaming*, to theatricality, indeed to the theatricality of the dream and the dream-work of theatricality – although it should be obvious enough by now that such 'dreaming' cannot simply be opposed to the ostensibly 'serious' and 'sober' efforts and activities of more 'reputable' scholars. Yet on the surface, at least, Weber's books and essays do seem much less performative or theatrical in style than, for example, Derrida's *Glas* or his writing on Mallarmé – so in what sense *exactly* are they 'theatrical'?

In 'Taking Place', Weber turns his attention to the Frankfurt Opera's staging of Wagner's *Ring of the Nibelung*. Here, his discussion draws upon Freud's conception, in the *Interpretation of Dreams*, of the 'navel of the dream', wherein:

> ... one notices a tangle of dream-thoughts arising which resists unravelling but has also made no further contributions to the dream-content. This then is the navel of the dream, the place where it straddles the unknown. The dream-thoughts to which interpretation leads one are necessarily intermin-able *and branch out in all directions into the netlike entanglement* of our world of thought. Out of one of the denser places in this network, the dream-wish rises like a mushroom out of its mycelium. (Cited in TP, 133)[4]

Dream-thoughts, as the *entstellte* 'fulfilment' of conflictual and hence unresolvable and ongoing desires, therefore unavoidably 'branch out in all directions'. They become an entangled and spreading expanse in which the dream-thoughts exceed their 'contributions to the dream-content', thereby inevitably dislocating the dream and its interpretation alike. As the 'netlike entanglement' thickens or intensifies, then, it also spills out and into 'our world of thought', as Freud puts it, and in particular, as Weber notes, into 'our waking thoughts' (TP, 133). Yet, if such a dislocating movement or process were permitted to continue without impediment, presumably the dream would become so swept into this 'navel' as to no longer simply 'straddle' the unknown. Instead, it would surely be entirely engulfed by it, to the point where even the most minimal degree of coherence or recognition would be lost. The dream would no longer be liable to any interpretation whatsoever. Equally, since the 'netlike entanglement' of dream-thinking would also engulf waking thought, nothing could stop conscious life becoming so drawn into the navel of the dream that it would be utterly incapable of establishing or maintaining any focus of attention. However, since (as Freud asserts) dreams do remain susceptible to interpretation, albeit of a specific and provisional kind, and since conscious life never seems to give itself over entirely to the 'navel of the dream', the dissipating movement of *Entstellung* must somehow be held in check. Freud's suggestion is therefore that this 'mycelium' not only proliferates and extends its 'netlike entanglement' but it in fact gives rise to a 'mushroom' – at last, a recognizable form found growing among this most fecund organic matter, somewhat akin to decomposing compost – to which Freud assigns the name of the 'dream-wish'. The dream-wish is, as Weber puts it, 'a new phenomenon rising above the proliferation of shadows to provide the badly needed bright new center of attention' (TP, 133). Yet, as Freud himself insists, the dream as the fulfilment of a wish cannot be construed in terms of the expression of a latent content, which might endow it with integrity as an intentional and objectifiable phenomenon. Rather, the dream-wish 'fulfils' itself only as it arises from the always conflictual and hence unresolvable play of desire(s) that give it its specific force or structure. As Weber tells us:

> The dream-wish, then, which arises out of the dream-navel, endows the interminable proliferation of dream-thoughts with a certain structure. But at the same time this structure recenters the dream around the 'unknown,' around the overdetermined conflictuality of which the dream is a self-dissimulating dissimulation. The emergence of the phallic dream-wish therefore does not abolish ... the thallic dynamics of the dream – it merely gives its dislocation a focus. (TP, 134)

Dream-thoughts (imbued with 'thallic dynamics' wherein, as the *OED* definition of 'thallus' suggests, the 'true roots are absent') unavoidably proliferate, spread, traverse and exceed their bounds, branching out and breaking into conscious life (as sensible, rational, voluntary ...). Yet the dissipating and decentring force of the dream-thought is somewhat held in check by what Weber calls a 'structure' or 'focus' conferred by the fulfilment of the dream-wish, which in turn 'recenters' the dream around the 'unknown', here conceived in terms of 'overdetermined conflictuality' and 'self-dissimulating dissimulation'. While the latter – 'self-dissimulating dissimulation' – recalls the irreducible *theatricality* of the dream, 'overdetermined conflictuality' takes place not only in the dream or the unconscious, but finds its way into 'waking thought' or conscious life – for example, in the conflictual play of forces that, as Weber's work shows us, give rise to technologies, 'works', institutions and interpretations of all kinds. The dislocating movement of *Entstellung* associated with dream-thoughts plays itself out, then, through the specific form – the 'mushroom' or reef – of the dream-wish, the fulfilment of which both decentres and recentres, structures and destructures the dream around the 'unknown' as the dream-navel, as the unconscious, as theatricality, as the 'overdetermined conflictuality' that gives rise to (always deconstructible) institution and interpretation.

As has already been noted, Weber's thinking and writing thereby cannot help but assume or partake of 'dream-thought', although, as should therefore be obvious, this could not just happen as the result of an intention, decision, strategy or rationale on Weber's part. As it branches out or breaks into conscious life, however, dream-thought not only submerges and sweeps focused or structured thinking into the entangled and dissipating space – the black hole – of the dream's navel. Instead, it gives rise to wishes which provide a 'center of attention', but one which nevertheless draws us back towards or into 'overdetermined conflictuality' and theatricality alike, and which therefore re-places or recentres this 'centre' around, or at the (decentring) limit of, the 'unknown'. While such 'themes' or 'ideas' could be said to constitute the abiding interest of Weber's work, explicit everywhere at the level of its 'content', it also seems fair to say that the very procedure or practice of this 'work' is bound up with the dislocating movement of *Entstellung*, a movement which we are here associating with both dream-thinking and theatricality. This *entstellte* 'work' of Samuel Weber could be described as a play or a 'goings-on' of destructuring structuration, in which the centre of attention is continually displaced, re-placed and displaced once more in turn, at – or, indeed, *as* – the very limit (never just a dividing line) of the 'other' or the 'unknown'. Just this *entstellte* participation on Weber's part means that each 'frame' calls for *another*, and *another* ('no glance can ever oversee') ... so that Weber's 'work' is itself *theatrical* in the sense of staging a 'series' of scenes that dislocate themselves and each other. In turn, this theatricality would disrupt or, indeed, dislocate any simple attempt to correlate, reduce and explain Weber's writings in terms of a continuous, consistent body of scholarship or a distinguished instance of philosophical 'development', accessible to its readership as an 'object' of knowledge or cognition to be grasped and mastered by an autonomous subject of reason or thought (the independent individual). The 'structure' or the 'focus' we might discern not only in particular texts by Weber, but linking his writings in general, undeniably reactivates the wish for a kernel or 'centre' (of attention) that is liable to interpretation. But such a 'centre' can be and is always dislocated or replaced by yet another frame, which in turn enters into the analysis only on condition of another (indeed, on the necessary yet impossible condition of a frame that must, in a sense, be *other* than the 'frame').

Hence, the reprises, repetitions, linkages and connections in Weber's work, to which the present study has, at times, drawn attention, constantly invite or require rephrasing, reiteration, reformulation – and hence, inevitably, transformation – of the questions or problems under discussion, undermining attempts at reduction, generalization, systematization or totalization. This 'invitation' to continually rephrase and reformulate is one to which I have attempted to respond, in following the dislocating movement of Weber's writings on a host of topics and issues including reading, interpretation, institution, psychoanalysis, technics, theatricality, deconstruction and so on.[5]

Theatricality and Uncanny Thinking

The second edition of Weber's *The Legend of Freud* includes a new essay, 'Uncanny Thinking', with which the book opens. Here, Weber describes his original project as an attempt to 'explore how Freud's writing and thinking are progressively caught up in what they set out primarily to describe and elucidate' (*LF*, 1). To this extent, the Freudian text continually calls into question the 'assumption of an extraterritorial position with respect to the matter being considered' (*LF*, 1). Detachment or 'safe distance' in regard to an object of interest, investigation or knowledge is jeopardized, for example, where either the patient or, indeed, the doctor comes to reject a perception that doesn't fit in with their expectations. Such a rejection does not amount simply to 'a *lack* of consciousness with respect to an object' (the object isn't just 'missed' or overlooked) but, more precisely, it entails 'a blindness of consciousness with respect to its own activity (of dissimulation)' (*LF*, 4). If what we are therefore describing is nothing other than the advent of the unconscious in conscious life, then here it is marked by a (re)doubling of consciousness's blindness – a blindness, that is, which can be described in terms of a twofold process that concerns both the inadmissible 'perception' which confronts consciousness to begin with and the dissimulating 'activity' of consciousness by which such a rejection remains unacknowledged. The unconscious, then, ushers in a scene that is characterized by relations of ambivalence, conflict and struggle, for here the subject is split off from itself, dispersed in an action which, while it may indeed be inaccessible to consciousness, nevertheless establishes the conditions for the emergence of a particular kind of *knowing*. And, far from being able simply to observe or comprehend such a phenomenon from the vantage-point of psychoanalytic interpretation or 'knowledge', Freud's own text implies that 'knowledge' itself may well be little more than the name we assign to the effort consciousness makes in trying to deal with processes it can never really come to master or, indeed, to *know*. This scenario, then, is one into which psychoanalysis itself must inevitably be drawn.

The rejection of a perception which doesn't fit in with one's expectations is, of course, how Freud tells the story of 'castration'. The perception of sexual difference is rendered compatible with the 'expectation' of male identity through the recounting of a story which, as Weber puts it, 'temporalizes' difference so as to redefine it 'as a modality of identity' (*LF*, 5). Hence, the immediate perception isn't merely rejected outright ('I must be wrong, there has to be a penis there'). Instead, the fact of sexual difference is rejected by way of recasting variation in terms of *lack*, so as to confirm the positive self-identity of the male ('there must have been a penis there once, I'm right after all'). Here, once more, the 'blindness' of the conscious mind can be described in terms of a double process which concerns, first of all, the inadmissible 'perception', but which also entails the dissimulating 'activity' of consciousness in relation to itself, by means of which the rejection remains unacknowledged *as such*, as it must do if the story of castration is to serve its purpose. And, as Weber points out, one of the main purposes of this story is to confirm the extraterritorial position of the storyteller himself. Since the story of castration is intended to render the perception of difference compatible with the narcissistic 'expectation' of a (male) self that wishes to consider itself 'intact, whole, autonomous' (*LF*, 6), then it is related precisely in order to propose that the ego can assume a position which is sufficiently separate and self-contained, in respect of the events being recounted, that it ultimately remains unaffected by them. 'The "I" that tells itself this story thereby strives to secure its position as mere "observer"', Weber tells us, 'situated at an ostensibly safe remove from the disturbing possibilities it seeks merely to describe or retell' (*LF*, 6). Yet while 'the separation it sought to dominate' is apprehended by this ego as something like 'an obstacle to be overcome', nevertheless as the trait of a rejected perception and, indeed, of consciousness's double and (re)doubling blindness, it remains as the 'constitutive force' of a self that is 'irrevocably scattered' and dispersed in the action or scene of the unconscious, from which the subject of the narrative or, indeed, of 'knowledge' can only *impossibly* hope to emerge unscathed.

This *other* story of 'castration', then, is best retold not in the idiom of theoretical description or positive, empirical knowledge, but via the language or thinking of the dream, with all the effects of theatricality that this entails ('the "I" of the dreamer ... finds itself scattered throughout the dream despite its apparent distance from it' (*LF*, 7)). Weber's 'Uncanny Thinking' therefore turns to E.T.A. Hoffman's uncanny tale, 'The Sandman', upon which Freud's essay on the uncanny concentrates. Here, then, one uncanny story, one (dream-) scene encounters another, or is staged within or alongside another.

And, perhaps, yet another, and, right here, look, another: my recounting of Weber's recounting of Freud's recounting of a tale by Hoffman which concerns ... recounting. But of what? As we shall see, the array of difficulties this very question occasions mean that these various retellings cannot so easily find a stable or secure 'center of attention' so as to be construed in terms of a series of concentric circles, each fully containing the other. Instead, our attention is drawn to the patterns of dislocation that repeat themselves throughout this 'series'.

Since, as Weber tells us, the Sandman 'names the violence of a certain disassemblage' (*LF*, 14), what we are doubtless in the midst of, here, is a retelling (*otherwise*) of the story of castration. (The Sandman eats dismembered parts of bodies, and his appearance 'medusizes' the transfixed child, whose gaze is itself threatened by the Sandman's particular taste for eating eyes.) But how is this story to be recounted, or *dreamt*, and by whom?

In Hoffman's tale, or rather within a letter to his fiancée's brother, the young student Nathanael conveys a recent, seemingly trivial occurrence, whereby an eyeglass vendor enters his lodgings, taking him unawares. Nathanael not only rejects the wares the eyeglass vendor offers him, but threatens him with violence unless he leaves immediately. By way of an explanation of his own, apparently excessive reaction, Nathanael recalls another scene, this time from his childhood, when his household was frequented by the portentous 'Sandman', whose identity remained a long while shrouded in mystery. Like the eyeglass vendor, then, the Sandman unexpectedly arrives upon the domestic scene (although he does so repeatedly) with a sudden, intrusive force which indicates the fragility of its defences and the vulnerability of its borders. If the coming of the eyeglass vendor only repeats this pattern of repetition, the fact that he nevertheless takes Nathanael unawares suggests the curious state of knowing *without* knowing that Freud associates with the subject who rejects a perception that doesn't fit in (the subject, for instance, of the story of castration). As a child, Nathanael responds to this threat by seeking, as Weber puts it, to *locate* it. (Indeed, several years later, he tries once again to overcome the intimidating episode of the eyeglass vendor's startling and unforeseen intrusion by locating it, this time in terms of his childhood memories which themselves only repeat, rather than resolve, the attempt to locate the threat.) This entails an effort to visualize the Sandman, to find out what he looks like. But, as Weber points out, 'the name and the story of the Sandman already anticipates this effort and incorporates it, as it were, into the threat' (*LF*, 8). For the very coming of the Sandman is marked not so much by his *appearance* (which, in any case, only threatens to devour the eye) as by an irresistible drift towards sleep and dreaming, one that is accompanied by the wholly unwelcome yet entirely irrepressible drawing down of heavy lids, which makes the child's eyes feel as though sand had been thrown into them.

To the extent that 'the very name and story of the Sandman' radically impedes the attribution of an origin or intention insofar as the meaning or identity of the Sandman is concerned – and indeed, since the story in fact reincorporates this very same effort so as to redouble the threat – the Sandman only *is* insofar as he is *coming*. Never does he *come*, arrive or *appear* definitively, once and for all (he will always come again, no doubt in unexpected guise); nor can his identity *as such* (for example, as a subject or agent in the traditional sense) ever be definitively postulated as anterior to the processes and effects that surround his coming. The Sandman's coming, then, powerfully recalls the comedic theatricality of the *posse* actor Beckmann, whose distinctive talent resides in his ability to 'come walking'. As we've seen, via Weber's work, Beckmann's theatrical style can be linked (perhaps by means of a kind of dream-thinking) to Derrida's 'vision' of the university after Kant, as an institution that is deeply unsure of its foundations and which therefore finds, founds and foots itself as a body continually off-balance. Such a university is therefore impelled to 'walk on two feet' (neither left nor right), in order to exert a kind of leverage on the basis of an 'other' that is not merely one of a pair. Beckmann's *coming*, then, could be taken to 'improvise the whole scenic setting' of the university institution after the Enlightenment. As a repetitious act without definitive origin or conclusion, his comically off-balance 'walking' repeats the coming of the Sandman, blinding the vision of, in this case, the university itself: as Derrida, following Heidegger, shows in 'The Principle of Reason: The University in the Eyes of its Pupils', the vision of the university proceeds from what remains concealed in that vision, since the institution built on the principle of reason is also constructed upon 'what remains hidden in that principle' (PR, 10).

Here, the strange familiarity and uncanny repetition that connects the Sandman and Beckmann might lead us to dream of new ways to reframe debates regarding the university institution – indeed concerning institutions of all kinds – in terms of the scene of the unconscious and the story of castration. For instance, we might then be able to retell *somewhat differently* the story of the 'impossible' emergence of knowledge from (the theatricality of) the dream. Equally, the *unheimlich* pathway that leads from Beckmann to the Sandman might allow us to restage the scene of the unconscious, and to recount the story of castration, in terms of the question of (the) institution – of psycho-analysis, for example. Here one finds an inextricable tangle of traits (Odradek) which one could never hope to exhaust or master. Each frame calls for another, dislocates and re-places itself and the other (or, indeed, 'in' the other) via a movement that continually circulates but never comes full circle, never allows us to achieve balance or completion. (Now I could speak of the extent to which Weber's own 'work' itself comes walking, in the style of Beckmann, or indeed just like the Sandman, in order to deal with all sorts of interesting and hitherto unforeseen consequences and effects that this might imply. But to take such a turn would only imply another frame, and 'who is to say where it starts, and where it stops?'.) In the midst of a kind of dream-thinking that leads us from the Sandman to Beckmann, then, we become drawn into the movement of destructuring structuration that we've associated with the theatricality of Weber's own writing, a theatricality which always leaves us teetering precariously at the limits of the unknown.

All this therefore compels us, somewhat off-balance, to somehow move, to take a plunge. So, if we return to the story that Weber is telling us (that Freud is telling us that Hoffman is telling us that Nathanael is telling us) pretty soon we're off elsewhere. Weber writes:

> The Sandman *is* insofar as he is *coming*. Nathanael's problem is related precisely to the ubiquitous possibility of this coming, an eventuality that cannot be foreclosed by any of the borders with which we seek to wall in our spaces and control access to them.
>
> The power of the Sandman, then, inheres in his ability to invade and occupy what in the modern period is considered the most sacred of spaces: the private space of the family, the *home*. At the same time, however, as he turns the home inside-out, he also reaffirms domestic space, but in a way that transforms it from a place of security... . (*LF*, 9)

By alluding to the Sandman's coming in terms of 'an eventuality that cannot be foreclosed by any of the borders with which we seek to wall in our spaces and control access to them', Weber recalls the 'goings-on' of technics, in which the unresolvable interplay of 'opening up' and 'closing down' puts *place* continually into *play*. Here, another frame suggests itself – only to open up the possibility of yet another, where 'the power of the Sandman' is associated with the ability to occupy so as to transform 'domestic space', calling to mind all that is involved, for Weber, in reading and writing—*chez* Derrida. Of course, in picking up these threads, a great deal more could be said on the subject of technics, interpretation, reading or indeed institution, in the context of this discussion of the uncanny, the unconscious and the story of castration. But whether we continue in this vein or that (and 'who is to say where it starts, and where it stops?'), the writing here suggests a variegated and proliferal structure or movement not dissimilar to the 'thallic dynamics of the dream'. And this entails a theatrical movement (uncanny thinking?) in which each scene is continually called into question, dislocated and re-placed, by an *other*.

But let's get back to the story once more. As we've said, the name and the tale of the Sandman together anticipate Nathanael's effort to visualize and hence definitively identify the threat he poses, and indeed such an effort is incorporated so as to redouble this threat (the child's eyes are transfixed by that which will medusize, blind or devour them). Far from becoming merely the object of an identification or recognition on the part of a detached observer who is placed, unseen, at a safe remove, the Sandman comes to confound or, rather, to disorganize the spectacle the child wishes to make of him; and it is therefore also in this sense that the Sandman 'names the violence of a certain disassemblage' akin to that of Ramades digging up the foundations of the operatic stage. Unable to maintain – or, indeed, to *stand* – the extraterritorial position of the unseen spectator, since it is his very *eyes* that the Sandman threatens to blind or devour, Nathanael is driven by the Sandman's 'appearance' to leap from his hiding place, to take the plunge 'from the ostensibly hidden and protected security of an unseen viewing position onto a stage whose borders are difficult to define, since they change in function of movements they cannot simply contain or situate' (*LF*, 14). As the Sandman takes centre stage, what actually *takes place* is, as we've seen, an indefinite and unpredictable number of shifts and repetitions (from the eyeglass vendor to the Sandman, from the Sandman to Beckmann, to Odradek, from Weber to Freud to Hoffman to Nathanael, from the story of castration and the scene of the unconscious to the advent of theatricality, to the question of institution, to the problem of technics, to that of reading and writing—*chez* Derrida, and so forth) which neither begin nor end with the Sandman's *coming*, and which therefore serve thoroughly to disorganize the borders of the stage he inhabits. And, at this point, where such a scene 'ceases to be mere story and spectacle and becomes a theatrical scenario instead' (*LF*, 14), the possibility that anyone could ever simply recount the tale falters. For who *could* recount it? Certainly not Nathanael, who, in taking the plunge, acts out his part in the story he otherwise wishes to relate and, indeed, interpret. Not Freud, who cannot exempt himself from rejecting those inadmissible perceptions which do not fit in with one's expectations and which therefore repeat themselves, in unexpected guise, precisely in the vicinity of consciousness's unacknowledged blindness (so that 'intellectual uncertainty' cannot be reduced merely to the 'anxiety' occasioned by the tale, as Freud would have us believe (*LF*, 15)). And not the Sandman, with whom the story never quite begins or ends. Not any one in the 'series' of storytellers – Weber, Hoffman, Freud, Nathanael, myself included – whose various recount-ings 'centre' upon a childhood memory which itself only repeats, rather than resolves, the attempt to locate and define the identity, intention or meaning of the Sandman. All of us, like Nathanael, take the plunge onto the stage, 'in both senses', as Weber tells us: 'taking a fall and being thrust or thrown off balance' (*LF*, 15). For this stage is itself the 'place' where the body 'as a matrix for the ego: self-contained, unified, integrated' (*LF*, 15) is violently disassembled or disorganized. Just as Nathanael's limbs are unscrewed, and his body dismembered, he therefore loses *consciousness* in a sudden spasm. The dream itself *theatrically* dislocates and re-places the conscious life – and hardly for Nathanael alone, but for anyone who would try to tell this story:

> Hidden behind his curtain, Nathanael believes he has discovered, with his own two eyes, just *who* the Sandman really *is*. He believes he has replaced the figurative destination 'Sandman' with an authentically proper name. But the name he comes up with turns out to be a link in a signifying chain that unravels what it is intended to close up: 'Coppelius' [the old laywer that occasionally dines with the family] becomes 'Coppola,' the vendor of *Perspektiven*, whose name ... signifies 'socket' or 'hollow,' but also recalls, phonetically, *copula*. The Sandman 'is' the lawyer who 'is(st) [or 'eats.'] The lawyer 'is' the vendor of prostheses, whose name recalls the operator of predication itself. But ... in thus consuming its univocal meaning, this *is(s)t* emerges as the disjunctive junction of that which diverges and yet coexists, as a part that never becomes a whole. (*LF*, 21)

Notes

1   Here Weber refers to Theodor Adorno's essay 'Opera', in *Introduction to the Sociology of Music*, trans. E.B. Ashton (New York: Seasbury, 1976), 71–84, esp. 81–82. He notes, however, that the passage quoted contains modifications to the translation of this text.
2   See S.E., 5, 506–507.
3   Ibid., 514.
4   Ibid., 530.
5   A further text of interest in regard to the question of theatricality in Weber's writing is his essay, 'Double take: acting and writing in Genet's "L'étrange mot d' ..." ', *Yale French Studies*, 91 (1997), 28–48. See also Weber's forthcoming book, *Theatricality as Medium*.

Conclusion

Taking Leave

Repetition, Recognition and Iterability

In his essay 'It', published in the fourth edition of *Glyph* in 1978, Weber discusses the dispute between Jacques Derrida and the speech act theorist John Searle over the term 'iterability'. Iterability, of course, engages questions concerning identity and repetition, and Weber's gloss on Derrida's usage of this term is as follows: 'If identity is a product of recognition, and hence of repetition, there is no consistent possibility of recognizing an identity independent of and prior to such repetition. Repetition will always exceed, qua possibility, its determination in terms of an object that is unique and self-contained' (I, 7). He goes on: 'Iterability, then, is what, for Derrida at least, precludes consciousness from ever becoming fully conscious of its object' or, indeed, of 'itself' (I, 7). For if 'something must be iterable in order to become an object of consciousness, then it can never be entirely grasped, having already been split in and by its being-repeated (or more precisely: by its *repeated being*)' (I, 7). The object of cognition thus 'recognized or understood' will therefore 'never be fully present to consciousness, nor entirely identical to itself' (I, 7).

The consequences of such iterability for a *theoretical* description or formulation (in any classical or traditional sense) of iterability 'itself' are, of course, not inconsiderable. As Weber puts it:

> ... the argument of iterability entails a peculiar and paradoxical difficulty. ... This difficulty may be formulated as follows: in order to speak about something called iterability, we must name it, identify it, describe it, and thereby treat it as though it were an object. In other words, we must conceive it in a way that it itself seems to call into question. (I, 8)

(It is worth recalling here that Weber refers to iterability by the nickname 'it', giving rise to highly charged linguistic inflections and multiplicities as one reads on.) In Derrida's terms, drawn from 'Signature Event Context', iterability's very 'structure' as one of (a) repetition that is never simply that of the Same, 'comports an internal and impure limit that prevents it from being identified, synthesized, or appropriated' (cited in I, 9).[1] It is, then, this 'internal and impure limit' which, as Weber tells us, 'makes iterability not simply a *term* designating an object that is self-contained, structured in and of itself, but rather "itself" a mark, a divided and divisive part of a movement that no one term can decisively determine, i.e. *terminate*' (I, 9). Drawing again on Derrida's own phraseology, from 'Signature Event Context', Weber writes: 'this is why this peculiar term refers not so much to a "structure" as to a "chain, since iterability can be supplemented by a variety of terms …"' (I, 9). Indeed, he goes further here than does Derrida, to insist that the term 'iterability' indeed *must* 'be substituted', displaced and dislocated as a term by *others*, if it is to avoid reduction to a repetition of the Same. Such necessary or unavoidable substitutions by *another* (and then another …) may be detected, of course, in the movement of theatricality, of aesthetic form, of technics, of debt, of institution and of reading, to which Weber's work devotes itself. Theatricality, technics, debt, institution, reading: all of these terms *must* be 'substitutes', and indeed *must* be 'substituted', in terms of the 'chain' of iterability. In(to) such a chain, therefore, iterability falls as a quasi-transcendental category: in a certain respect, it is just a part of the 'chain' it would otherwise seem to name in its entirety, thus re-marking itself as 'a divided and divisive part of a movement that no one term can decisively determine, i.e. *terminate*'. (The chain is, in a sense, broken (into) by what would seem to be its strongest or its most defining link: at any rate, this is what stops the chain ever quite coming full circle.) Henceforth, such 'supplementation' or 'substitution' cannot simply be thought to confine itself within the limits of the 'subject-matter' to which Weber devotes special attention. That is, it (iterability) falls short of defining the thematic consistency of self-contained 'objects' of inquiry and cognition (the 'topics' on which Weber writes); or of allowing the possibility of a recognition of the repetition of the Same as one explores linkages within the 'chain' (moving between Weber's writings on psychoanalysis, institutions, technics, media, aesthetics, theatricality and so forth). For such patterns of recognition would presuppose and reduce 'iterability' or 'supplementarity' or 'substitution' as mere 'objects'. The classical notion of the 'object', of course, implies a clear-cut distinction whereby the 'object' *is one* insofar as it is present to a *subject*: a consciousness that is fundamentally self-contained and self-identical, extrinsic and autonomous in relation to the 'objects' it seeks to apprehend. If iterability 'is what, for Derrida at least, precludes consciousness from ever becoming fully conscious of its object or of itself', then other terms in the 'chain' – theatricality, for example, or debt – divide and dislocate the subject so that it 'itself' becomes 'a divided and divisive part of a movement' which can no more be simply recognized than it can be determined or controlled. Let us only recall, for instance, Nathanael's leap, or 'Derrida's' joke. Indeed, it is for similar reasons that one could say of Weber's writing that it does not simply seek to describe problematical aspects of our traditional conceptions of the 'author' and the 'work', but that it 'itself' is taken up and transformed by the very movement (of iterability's 'chain') that brings these conceptions into question, so that it *assumes* this movement in the very 'act' of seeking to describe it (an 'act', however, which can never quite *be one*, an object that never quite *is one*, an assumption which is never quite that of a conscious intention, but, more likely, of a debt, a joke, a leap, with all the ambivalent and unpredictable effects this entails).

Taking and Leaving

In an essay entitled 'Literary Study in the Transnational University', J. Hillis Miller also revisits the encounter of Derridean deconstruction with the speech act theory of Searle and of his forebear J.L. Austin. Miller reminds us that, for Austin, a speech act 'depends for its efficacy on an elaborate context of protocols, rules, institutions, roles, laws, and established formulae. These need to be in place before the performative utterance is made' (LS, 179). In this perspective, comprehensibility therefore depends on a complexly preconstituted framework establishing the conditions of formulation, transmission and reception of any communication. The Austinian conception of a speech act also presupposes, of course, the pre-existence of a self as agent able to recognize, comprehend or *apprehend* (in at least a double sense: to understand, but also to *grasp* and *arrest*) the 'context' in which speech acts can thereby 'meaningfully' take place. Unsurprisingly, therefore, speech act theory *simply cannot understand* iterability as a situation in which the 'object' of cognition or communication can neither be 'fully present to consciousness, nor entirely identical to itself', as Weber puts it.

In contrast, then, Miller describes an 'alternative kind of performative' that is of interest to deconstruction, one which paradoxically 'creates the norms and laws that validate it'. Each such performative 'constitutes a happening that changes decisively the surrounding context. It responds to a call or demand from an "other" that can never be institutionalized or rationalized' (LS, 179). Hence the call of the 'other', which in this formulation brings the speech act into being, would have to pre-exist or, at any rate, exceed any set 'context' that might be *apprehended* by a subject or agent of cognition or communication. In affirming that the very idea of a speech *act* is therefore a catachresis according to this formulation of performativity, Miller is called on to quote Derrida: 'As Derrida puts it, such a speech act is a catachresis that "while continuing to work through tradition emerges at a given moment as a *monster*, a monstrous mutation without tradition or normative precedent"' (LS, 179).[2]

How might deconstruction not only affirm but also engage in just such an 'alternative kind of performative'? Such a problem obviously re-engages the question of how iterability might be *taken up* or how it might *take hold* in the very midst of those writings that seek to devote attention to *it*; how such writings might be forced to *take their leave* just while getting '*a take*' on or coming to *feel more at home with* iterability. And, in a way that is not dissimilar to the situation of reading, of debt, of the leap or of the joke, we might wonder about the effects of such 'scenic inscription' (to borrow a Weberian term) in the conflictual force-field of the 'object', and the kinds of scenarios it entails or implies.

At this point, by your leave, so near the end, I would like to take the liberty of departing from the 'work' of the 'author' Samuel Weber, if only to show – yet again, via *another* – how such departing or *leave-taking* is both impossible and necessary. For, if nothing else, iterability entails a certain sort of de-parting or de-part-ure: that is, a divided, redoubling movement which repeats as it separates, returning *as* leaving.

One response to the kinds of question outlined above might be sought in the vicinity of Derrida's own remarks concerning the status of his written texts and spoken lectures as a form of *teaching*. The very idea of teaching obviously reintroduces the sorts of question associated with iterability: those of communicability, repetition, recognition, knowl-edge, identity, intentionality, authority – all major concerns of Weber. And, of course, many of Derrida's published writings have often stemmed from work done in seminars or lectures given on specific occasions, with the singular and performative aspects of such events often being carefully preserved and, indeed, presented as a condition of the thinking that takes shape in these various texts. But let us look at merely one example. At the beginning of 'Otobiographies', itself a text originally presented as a lecture at the University of Montreal in 1979 and followed by round-table discussions in which a select assembly of distinguished colleagues participated, Derrida prefaces his treatment of certain texts by Nietzsche with the following remarks:

> I would like to spare you the tedium, the waste of time, and the subservience that always accompany the classic pedagogical procedures of forging links, referring back to prior premises or arguments, justifying one's own trajectory, method, system, and more or less skillful transitions, reestablish-ing continuity, and so on. These are but some of the imperatives of classical pedagogy with which, to be sure, one can never break once and for all. Yet, if you were to submit to them rigorously, they would very soon reduce you to silence, tautology, and tiresome repetition. (O, 3–4)

These remarks, concerning the characteristic linkages, repetitions and 'transitions' normally expected from a scholarly body of work, may well establish a pertinent setting within which to consider once more the distinctive movement or procedure of Weber's own writings and, indeed, that of the present study. Be that as it may, Derrida's apparent tone here belies the emergence of a quite significant line of thinking. For Derrida, it is neither that the academic conventions of a more or less orthodox pedagogy can simply be ignored, surpassed or abandoned, nor that they permit themselves to be unquestioningly defended and thereby unproblematically reproduced. Rather, any teaching necessarily partaking of pedagogical tradition that tries nonetheless to remain wholeheartedly devoted to an unsupplemented reinscription or conservation of the method or the system that allows and enables it to set out will inevitably dwindle into circularly self-justifying practices that actually inhibit and eventually preclude everything to do with the *event* of (a) teaching: of teaching as a singularly performative activity and a finally incalculable form of address to – but, perhaps more so, *from* – the other. One can therefore neither simply take nor leave 'classic pedagogical procedures', and in fact one must to some extent both take (partake of) and leave them at one and the same time in order for teaching to take place at all.

On closer inspection, then, Derrida's remarks would in fact seem to raise important questions concerning the possibility of a responsible standpoint on quite difficult and complex matters. In the face of this complication of otherwise easily polarizable positions on the issue of pedagogical tradition, Derrida therefore proposes a 'compromise' to his audience. This has to do with a deconstructive procedure that presents its practitioner as engaged in some sort of settling of accounts on a number of problems (however ironic or impossible this may seem, it is of course also unavoidable), rather than aspiring to the teaching of 'truth' as such. Derrida anticipates that, for some, such an approach will seem too 'aphoristic or inadmissible', while others will accept it as 'law', and yet others will 'judge [it] to be not quite aphoristic enough' (O, 4). While it would be easy enough to translate such categorizations into very familiar groupings, perspectives or positions regarding Derridean deconstruction in general, what is perhaps more interesting here is that, on the basis of just this 'compromise', whereby deconstruction presents itself as neither just entirely inside nor outside 'classical pedagogy', Derrida begins to question or, one might even say, *recalculate* the possibilities of what is called 'academic freedom' in the very process of what would seem to be an appeal to it.

Derrida insists that, since he does not wish to 'transform myself into a diaphanous mouthpiece of eternal pedagogy' (O, 4), a fountain of self-proclaimed truth, untrammelled authority and self-sustaining mastery (Derrida himself already having indicated the inevitable atrophying of any such teaching, although also its unavoidable persistence to some extent), his 'compromise' or procedure is therefore one that would seem to somewhat liberate his audience or the 'students' of his teaching, so that 'whoever no longer wishes to follow may do so' (O, 4). 'As everyone knows, by the terms of *academic freedom* – I repeat: a-ca-dem-ic free-dom – you can take it or leave it', he says (O, 4). Here, Derrida not only alerts our attention to the somewhat contradictory elements inscribed within our usual evocations of pedagogical tradition, which stress both teacherly authority and freedom of inquiry. More than this, a certain ironic tone becomes evident, underlying what seems to be a quite deliberately *repeated* emphasis on academic freedom itself. For Derrida has already shown that any worthwhile teaching (such as deconstruction, for instance), positioned in an ambivalent or equivocal relation to 'classical pedagogy', neither simply frees nor binds the event or activity of (a) teaching in relation to (a) tradition. Derrida's (teaching of) deconstruction in regard to the teaching of Nietzsche (the 'topic' of 'Otobiographies') obviously cannot offer a straightforward choice to the audience or student (or reader) of Derrida, between unincumbered intellectual freedom, on the one hand, or absolute bondage to pedagogical mastery, on the other. Just as Derrida, by his own admission, can neither simply take nor leave 'classical pedagogy', and (for that matter) since any teaching worth the name must both take and leave it simultaneously, so those that hear Derrida speak at Montreal in 1979 would, similarly, finally be bereft of any such choice forming the basis of a conventional appeal to academic freedom. To agree with everything Derrida would have to say, to 'take' deconstruction in undiluted form, would be to absolutely submit to and thereby necessarily obliterate its teaching – that is, ultimately, *to take leave of it*. (This would amount to misunderstanding it (iterability) on condition of understanding, recognizing, apprehending it entirely.) On the other hand, to absolutely reject or wholly take issue with, to entirely take leave of Derrida's discussion or approach from the outset would necessitate, quite impossibly, either a complete departure from the conventions of academic exposition which Derrida insists constitute the minimal level of intelligibility of his (or indeed any other) learned address, or otherwise would manifest an absolute defence of 'classical pedagogy' – in which case any dispute with Derrida, any supposed 'taking leave' of him, could never take the form of an absolutely diametrical opposition, for reasons he himself already presupposes and makes clear. (Or, in different terms, to radically *misunderstand* Derridean deconstruction, to reduce it as an 'object' to the status or image of mere unintelligibility, would far from guarantee the standpoint of a complete remove from iterability – or indeed from *reading*, joking, the debt or the leap, all of which substitute themselves as parts of iterability's 'chain'.) One can therefore never simply 'take it or leave it' in regard to this lecture by Derrida, or for that matter in regard to the teaching of deconstruction, perhaps even teaching itself, in general.

Thus, it is not just that 'classical pedagogy' and 'academic freedom' as clearly identifiable categories or forms constitute contradictory or somewhat opposed elements that vie with one another, bringing an awkward tension to bear on accepted notions and norms concerning scholarly tradition and convention. Rather, it is that *both* 'academic freedom' and 'classical pedagogy' are themselves traversed or cross-cut by differential traits that actually, paradoxically bind them together according to the logic of the supplement, of the remainder, or of the double bind.

It is this kind of recognition that orients Derrida's reading of Nietzsche's *On the Future of Our Educational Institutions* (1872). Here, Derrida observes that Nietzsche's recommendation of the very strictest linguistic discipline, 'as a counter to the kind of "academic freedom" that leaves students and teachers free to their own thoughts or programs', is not intended simply to 'set constraint over against freedom' (O, 33). Rather, for Nietzsche, it is possible to discern a more fundamental type of constraint underlying conventional appeals to academic freedom in the university – one which consists precisely in the fact that such constraint, as Derrida puts it, 'conceals and disguises itself in the form of laisser-faire' (O, 33). 'Through the said "academic freedom," it is the State that controls everything' Derrida remarks in discussing Nietzsche's text. 'In fact', he notes, 'the autonomy of the university, as well as of its students and professor inhabitants, is a ruse of the State.' From this point of view, 'Nietzsche's lectures can thus be read as a modern critique of the cultural machinery of the State and of the educational system that was, even in yesterday's industrial society, a fundamental part of the State apparatus' (O, 33). Such a perspective, emerging here from 'Otobiographies', might be linked to Derrida's discussion of a statist problematics of education after the Enlightenment, which Derrida himself associates with one of the principal proper names in the philosophical tradition – namely, Hegel. A fuller discussion of this problematics, found in the essay 'The Age of Hegel', is one in which Derrida undertakes a patient and detailed historico-sociological analysis of the complex interplay between particular kinds of liberal and enlightened discourse on the one hand, and, on the other, the 'mobile, subtle, sometimes paradoxical dynamic' of the given forces of civil society that in fact also emanate from, flow into and circulate within certain missives Hegel writes to a representative body of the Prussian State: the Ministry of Spiritual, Academic and Medical Affairs – which Derrida terms a 'State bureaucracy in the process of organizing the nationalization of the structures of philosophical education by extracting it, based upon a historical compromise, from clerical jurisdiction' (AH, 4). This is a correspondence, then, in which one can detect a very (or, indeed, over-) determined discourse concerning educational institutions 'in the age of European civil service' (AH, 11), as Derrida puts it, being traversed by the differential traits that organize and distribute the complex relations of academic freedom and institutionalized constraint within an emerging statist rationale taking shape in the wake of the Enlightenment.

Deconstruction's reading of the philosophical tradition's relation to educational institutions and their statist problematics in the age of Enlightenment therefore establishes a setting in which Nietzsche's (and, indeed, Derrida's) suspicion of any simple appeal to 'academic freedom' might be understood in terms of a rigorous rethinking of the complexly intertwined relations between academic freedom, orthodox pedagogy and politico-institutional constraints. We cannot just 'take' or 'leave' these phenomena, their concepts and effects, without such a rethinking – which itself would neither simply partake nor take leave of them. One important implication here might be that the aporetical condition of (a) teaching (of deconstruction, for example), whereby one can neither simply *take it* nor *leave it*, itself provides a setting in which to use deconstruction – even as it thinks the *prehistory* of 'postmodernity' or 'globalization' – a prehistory that is obviously entwined with the era of the nation-state, the traditions of which, however, one might nevertheless neither simply *take* nor *leave*, to imagine the kind of dissensual academic community advocated recently by critics such as Bill Readings and J. Hillis Miller. This would be a community not simply bounded by a horizon of consensus and sustained by the sort of communicative rationality advocated by the German Idealists or, more recently, Habermasian thought, nor would it be a community underpinned by freedom of dissent as a notion indissociable from traditional claims to academic freedom – a notion which in fact presupposes at the more fundamental level an entirely common and shared understanding of academic protocols and conventions. A dissensual 'community', then, would offer neither the possibility of harmonious belonging nor that of absolute separation or opposition. Dissensus of the kind that leaves all those engaged in the scene of teaching unable simply either to *take it* or *leave it* obviously implies a complicated network of relations and obligations which nevertheless *leaves open* the question of (among other things) responsibility or, indeed, that of the 'ethical', precisely because, in the very event of teaching, such a question remains irreducible to the rationality and rational ground of autonmuous subjects, or of the autonomous subject.

The remarks that inaugurate Derrida's 'Otobiographies' might therefore amount to an 'alternative kind of performative' of the sort described by Miller, in the sense that, 'while continuing to work through tradition', what 'emerges at a given moment' does so as 'a *monster*, a monstrous mutation without tradition or normative precedent'. Precisely by 'continuing to work through tradition', deconstruction here nevertheless gives rise to 'mutations' (*leaving* as *taking*, *taking* as *leaving*) that also interrupt or exceed (rather than just dispense with) 'tradition' or 'normative precedent'. But the word *monster*, italicized for emphasis by Derrida here, must surely be seen as a strong and somewhat shocking term to deploy when describing such 'mutations'. Does deconstruction in its teaching or *as* a teaching really give rise or give birth to *monsters*? What can the 'monstrous' or the 'monster' really mean, raising its head or its hand (or turning an 'other' ear, the ear of the other) in the midst of deconstruction's teaching?

In 'What is Called Thinking?' Heidegger embarks on a thought of the gift and a thought of the hand that would in turn render thinking itself irreducible to the dictates of utility, trade and technics that in various ways underpin all activity governed by the requisites of capital. Obviously this thought of the gift and of the hand would therefore necessitate, in this very same setting, a thinking of the problem of university teaching itself. Heidegger writes: 'The hand reaches and extends, receives and welcomes – and not just things: the hand extends itself, and receives its own welcome in the hand of the other. The hand keeps. The hand carries. The hand designs and signs, presumably because man is a (monstrous) sign'.[3] In establishing some sort of relation between 'man' and monstrosity, this passage provides the basis for a number of reflections that arise in Derrida's essay, '*Geschlecht* II: Heidegger's Hand'. Here, Derrida evokes and explores the weight and burden of the word *Geschlecht* in regard to the German philosophical tradition after the Enlightenment, and particularly in relation to the work of Heidegger himself. For Derrida, *Geschlecht* is a more or less untranslatable term that nevertheless variously comes to mean 'sex, race, species, genus, gender, stock, family, generation or genealogy, community' (*G*, 162), according to a number of somewhat fraught contexts that determine its sense and usage at different moments in this tradition. In broader terms, then, Derrida is seeking in this essay to embark once more on a series of reflections concerning philosophical nationality and nationalism in German, not least as part of a serious engagement with the problem of Heidegger's relation to Nazism that is to some extent put aside here, but treated more fully in texts such as *Of Spirit*. Derrida negotiates the term *Geschlecht*, therefore, in order to try to think and move among various notions of belonging that, in the German philosophical tradition since the Enlightenment, determine different accounts of the national (both in the sense of national and of racist or biologistic ideologies), as well as accounts of linguistic idiomaticity, and of the relations of humanity and animality that might also be taken to determine belonging where *Geschlecht* is concerned. It goes without saying that, for any essay which wants to evoke the topic of (the politics of) Heidegger's teaching (including, since it could hardly be excluded, the Rectoral Address of 1933) and its relation to a wider philosophical tradition, these are very deep waters indeed. Nevertheless, if it is possible both to recognize and set aside for a moment the obvious political stakes of any such discussion, one interesting aspect of Derrida's essay is the way in which it takes a number of Heidegger's texts to provide a setting for a closely woven set of questions having to do with nationhood, humanistic learning, the *Geschlecht* of the human, and the monstrosity of 'man' in the hand that signs, carries, extends itself to the other and (thereby relatedly) teaches. These questions would clearly impose themselves on the issue of the future of the university and the humanities, and of the (ruined) relations of teaching, learning, culture, community and nation-state in the age of technological reproducibility and global capital – issues that have so interested critics like Samuel Weber, Bill Readings and J. Hillis Miller in recent times.

Heidegger's hand – the hand that raises its head or hand in 'What is Called Thinking?' – is avowedly monstrous. This is the hand that crafts, gives, signs and teaches in ways that interrupt or exceed all the various activities that characterize the bureaucratic and technocratic regimes of the modern university as the place of science and technics serving the wider interests of capital. But, asks Derrida:

> Why 'monster'? ... What is *un monstre*? You know the polysemic gamut of this word, the uses one can make of it, for example concerning norms and forms, species and genus/gender: thus concerning *Geschlecht*. I shall begin by privileging here another course [*direction*]. It goes in the direction, the *sens*, of a less known sense, since in French *la monstre* (a changing of gender, sex, or *Geschlecht*) has the poetico-musical sense of a diagram that *shows* [*montre*] in a piece of music the number of verses and the number of syllables assigned to the poet. *Monstrer* is *montrer* (to show or demonstrate) ... *Le monstre* or *la monstre* is what shows in order to warn or put on guard. (*G*, 166)

In the very context of questions of 'norms and forms', of belonging and community – questions that have imposed themselves within and upon the thinking of the academic community ever since the days of German Idealism – Derrida finds a particular sense or type of monstrosity inscribed within the very discourse or thinking of *Geschlecht*. Here, to show, to demonstrate, to alert attention, to warn, to instruct or to *teach* is monstrous. Why, monstrous? Turning to part of a well-known poem by Holderlin, 'Mnemosyne', to which Heidegger returns in 'What is Called Thinking?', Derrida gives us Holderlin to read via the translation by Becker and Granel, the translators into French of 'Was heisst Denken?':

> We are a 'monster' void of sense
> We are outside sorrow
> And have nearly lost
> Our tongue in foreign lands.

Leaving aside that which would lead him back too rapidly to questions of nationality and nationalism, Derrida concentrates on the '"we, monster"' of this evocation (*G*, 167). (Here, it should be noted that certain effects attend his decision to read the French translation, since 'Ein Zeichen sind wir, deutungslos', the line from the poem on which Derrida concentrates, is more frequently translated as 'we are a meaningless sign'. The sign may be not just meaningless but also 'monstrous', yet it is surely monstrous *as* sign.) Whether this 'we' to whom Derrida draws our attention is taken to indicate 'man', 'humanity', 'nation' or some or other sense of *Geschlecht*, the monster that signs, 'shows' or 'warns', is singularly striking:

> ... since, showing, signifying, designating, this sign is void of sense (*deutungslos*). It says itself void of sense ... we are sign – showing, informing, warning, pointing as sign toward, but in truth toward nothing, a sign out of the way ... in a gapped relation to the sign ... display [*montre*] that deviates from the display or monstration, a monster that shows [*montre*] nothing. This gap of the sign to itself and to its so-called normal function, isn't it already a monstrosity of monstrasity ... a monstrosity of monstration? (*G*, 167)

Setting to one side the various ways in which Derrida tries to locate this interrelation of monstrosity and sign in the broader framework of the development of Heidegger's thought, the monstrosity of the sign as described here would seem to resonate with and reinvoke precisely the 'alternative kind of performative' outlined by Miller. Instead of just pointing towards and remaining in the grip of 'an elaborate context of protocols, rules, institutions, roles, laws, and established formulae' which, in rather static ways, 'need to be in place before the performative utterance is made', this alternative kind of performative 'creates the norms and laws that validate it' and thereby necessarily shows in the (monstrous) form of showing nothing. Such monstration is therefore monstrous in the 'gapped relation' of the sign to itself and to its 'so-called normal function', which, of course, has to do with the logics of presence and reference. Paradoxically, however, this monstration would at the same time obviously continue 'to work through tradition' (to borrow Derrida's phrase), since Derrida himself shows how the very question of monstration and monstrosity arises in the vicinity of questions of *Geschlecht* (of belonging and community, of (national) culture, of species and genus, of 'man', humanity and animality, and of 'norms and forms') that not only characterize a long-standing philosophical tradition, but that may even be thought to supply the very conditions of possibility for a thinking and realization of the Enlightenment university itself. Akin to the idea of 'monstration' which Derrida pursues via a reading of Heidegger's essay, then, the 'alternative kind of performative' Miller associates with Derridean deconstruction would similarly work 'through' tradition – here, more specifically, a tradition of *Geschlecht* or 'belonging' to be discerned both in the 'ruins' and in the 'remains' of the university today. Yet it is important to recall that the performativity we are associating with the (Heideggerian) hand that shows and teaches as a de(con)struction of tradition is one that, nonetheless, 'emerges at a given moment as a *monster*, a monstrous mutation without tradition or normative precedent' (to reprise Derrida once again). Not only would this facilitate (or, indeed, render inevitable) 'mutations' proliferating in excess of the bureaucratizing and rationalizing forces of the scientific and technocratic university and indeed, the legacies of 'belonging' that are tied to notions of (national) culture. It would also give a clue and a cue to the aporetical problem of teaching deconstruction as unavoidably the teaching of that which, caught within the (broken) clasp of iterability's 'chain', nevertheless remains virtually unteachable *as such*.

Such monsters as we are describing are the monsters of man or of man's hand. Not least, this is insofar as they both embody 'otherwise' and thoroughly deform the various projects of *Geschlecht* which in fact underpin the essential traditions of the university and of the nation-state since the Enlightenment. These manmade monsters, monsters of man, might be taken and affirmed as fertile mutations that productively distort the longstanding endeavours of humanistic study. Examples of such mutations, of such monsters (giving-taking-leaving-belonging) may perhaps abound just where (the) teaching (of) deconstruction 'takes place' in the university's remains.

Notes

1 Weber here refers to Jacques Derrida, 'Signature Event Context', *Glyph*, 1, 210.
2 Miller here quotes from Jacques Derrida, 'Deconstruction and the Other', in R. Kearney (ed.), *States of Mind: Dialogues with Contemporary Thinkers* (New York: New York University Press, 1995), 123.
3 Quoted in Jacques Derrida's '*Geschlecht* II: Heidegger's Hand', in *Deconstruction and Philosophy: The Texts of Jacques Derrida*, ed. J. Sallis (Chicago, Il and London: University of Chicago Press, 1987), 161–96 at 168.

Responding: A Discussion with Samuel Weber

The following interview was conducted by e-mail correspondence during September 2001. On 11 September, the World Trade Centre in New York was destroyed and the Pentagon badly damaged by a series of attacks. The participants in the discussion (Samuel Weber, Simon Morgan Wortham, together with Gary Hall of the University of Middlesex) felt compelled to respond to these events. In what follows, immediate reactions to the attacks and subsequent developments as they unfolded therefore contend – perhaps uneasily, but also perhaps productively – with a series of reflections on Weber's thinking, writing and critical practice over a number of years. What characterizes the discussion overall, in terms both of its 'content' and its very 'taking place', is the question of a critical or 'theoretical' discourse acting itself out in relation to a series of phenomena, acts or events to which it is bound to respond. It is a matter of judgement whether this distinctive and distinguishing trait of the discussion pulls it apart, or whether in some way it pulls it together. But such a characteristic trait nevertheless engages a whole set of questions and problems (to do with repetition, singularity, the uncanny and so forth) which in turn might be taken as characteristic of the work of Samuel Weber. Questions and responses have been dated to preserve and to highlight the temporal dimension of the 'event' – both of the interview taking place, and of the occurrences happening on an international scale that the discussion could not help but address.

Simon Morgan Wortham and Gary Hall (10 September 2001)

Samuel Weber, taking into account a large body of work written over a number of years, the range and scope of your interests is obviously very varied and broad. For instance, you write on psychoanalysis, literature, philosophy, aesthetics, the media, technics and technology, institutions, and theatre. And yet what is striking is the extent to which certain texts, readings and critical moves tend to be revisited or replayed on a variety of different occasions. To take just one example: you return more than once to the question of aesthetic and reflective judgement in Kant, to show how, in this part of Kant's critical philosophy, cognition and judgement take place on condition of an *other*. From this point onwards, you are able to discuss problems of aesthetic form, of parergon and institution, and of the 'fateful and ambiguous legacy' that Kant bequeaths to the institution of the humanities. But this reading also allows you to suggest that such processes or operations of cognition tend to theatricalize knowledge, to transform the grounds of knowledge into a rather more unsteady (or, even, comedic) platform upon which we witness certain styles of mimicry being performed or staged. Here, then, the ambivalence that attends humanistic knowledge seems to rest upon a question of theatre. Furthermore, in *Mass Mediauras*, the Kantian problem of aesthetic judgement would in turn appear to set off your work on Heidegger and his account of the 'goings-on' of technics. In this context, technological understanding, activity and development depend on very ambivalent processes of securing and unsecuring that begin to unravel as man endeavours to 'gain a stand' and to 'establish himself' by means of the knowledge of beings that Heidegger calls *techné*. Technological man thus orients himself in a way that begins to look rather theatrical and, to go further, perhaps even spectacularly comedic. Such a problem of orientation, then, connects a discussion of technics and technology to problems of cognition and judgement, to questions of aesthetics and form, to the matter of theatre and, indeed, to the problematics of institution. In returning to a particular text or reading, then, such connections, reorientations or transformations obviously emerge in a way that powerfully assumes and replays the problematics of repetition and iterability that are discussed in a number of places in your work. Here, the relationship between what is singular and what is universal becomes very complicated, to say the least. But perhaps you might care to say something more explicit about the conceptual grounds of the key 'terminology' you deploy: for example, 'technics', 'ambivalence', 'institution', 'theatre'. Is it at all possible that the rereadings or repetitions that characterize your work rest upon any kind of quasi-transcendental term or terms? Would this be a source of orientation? How else might you describe what is going on when one begins to have the – perhaps uncanny – experience of going over 'familiar ground' in your writing?

Samuel Weber (10 September 2001)

Your question, which addresses the 'uncanny', is itself not a little uncanny, at least for me. Especially since I'm sure that however I respond, I won't be able to avoid a certain repetition, and hence doubtless a certain 'familiarity'. Let's hope it's an uncanny one.

Nietzsche, who together with Kierkegaard placed the question of repetition, recurrence, *Wiederkehr* on the agenda – Nietzsche writes somewhere that with passing years one finds oneself returning to certain questions that seem to change very little over time. These questions, which function as a kind of bedrock of identity, are more difficult to 'lose' than to retain. Whether this 'bedrock' becomes a source of strength and discovery, or a prison, depends on how those questions 'return': whether they primarily only 'determine', in the simply restrictive sense of setting limits, or whether the limits they trace gesture towards a space not simply contained within the area they demarcate. This is one of the reasons why a sense of the 'uncanny' – indeed an openness to it – is indispensable, if one is to avoid the kind of entropy that a purely obsessive recurrence would entail.

There certainly is a dimension of 'familiarity' in my writings, but I try to think of it, to relate to it, as something other than a simple ground. Although I hesitate to limit it to a single name, if I were forced to, I would take the one, or rather, the series you have mentioned and I have begun to extend: 'repetition', 'iterability' and so on as themselves 'uncanny' questions, and as the question of the uncanny. This set or series of related (but not identical) terms marks a certain discovery, an 'experience' in the sense of *Erfahrung*, traversal or trajectory, 'peripeteia without anagnoresis' to vary the Aristotelian formula. Or perhaps, thinking of Beckett, 'anagnoresis as peripeteia', a formula for the uncanny recognition of something that, in being the same, reveals itself to be different.

In the course of my thinking, that trajectory begins with Adorno's condemnation of the *Immergleiche* – of that which is 'ever-the-same' – as a form of repetition, through Freud's 'repetition compulsion' that is both 'always the same' and yet never entirely appropriable, to Derrida's use of repetition to deconstruct the Husserlian notion of 'ideality' as the monological (and prelinguistic) discourse of the soul with itself (in *Speech and Phenomenon*). 'Repetition' has, it seems, haunted me for a long time, first in the guise of a polemical object of criticism (Adorno, Marcuse), then as a problematic discovery (Freud) leading to an even more problematic hypothesis ('the death-drive'), and finally – but, of course, there is no finality here, only finitude – to Derrida's compelling formulation of iterability in 'Signature Event Context' and *Limited Inc*. It has also haunted me via Kierkegaard's theatricalization of *Gjentagelsen* – which means 'taking again' ('reprise' is the provocative rendering of a recent French translation). This recurrence of the motif of 'repetition' has been more than a question – over the years. Rather, it has become a challenge to which I have had little choice but to respond.

Repetition is therefore a challenge for me, in the sense that it defies whatever I thought I understood by the word. Of this challenge, let me just mention two interrelated aspects. First, that, as Kierkegaard – or rather, as Constantin Constantius, the narrative figure who fictionalizes authorship in *Gjentagelse* – states, repetition, in contrast to recollection (anamnesis), is directed towards the future, not towards the past. That certainly doesn't make sense, not at first sight at least. Which is why it is interesting, and challenges one to think further. Second, the difference, on which Derrida in his debate with Searle insists, between 'iterability' and 'iteration' (or, if you will, between 'repeatability' and 'repetition'): the difference between something that simply 'is', whose mode of being can be adequately articulated in the present indicative – iteration – as an act or occurrence that is present-to-itself, and something that 'exists', if it exists at all, as a kind of possibility (in *Limited Inc*. Derrida calls it a 'structural possibility'). A 'kind of possibility' in the sense of one that is no longer defined by the oppositional logic of identity, which is to say, as being the opposite of 'reality' or 'actuality' (the difference between these two terms can be ignored in our context). For what distinguishes iterability from iteration is that it does not necessarily imply or entail the possibility of its enactment: it entails a possibility that is not a sub-species or dialectical other of 'reality' as self-fulfilment, actualization or self-presence. Or, to use a category that has proved useful for me over the years, as a form of self-containment. Hence, for Derrida, iterability, far from designating a possible realization, is 'actually' much closer to 'impossibility', inasmuch as its mode of being is such that it never fully 'takes place', a process that Derrida early on associated with a certain 'theatricality' (my term, not necessarily his): for instance, in his reading of Mallarmé's short text, *Mimique* (in *La double séance*, 'The Double Session').

This conjugation of 'possibility' and 'impossibility' as non-exclusive, and indeed as convergent (although again, as not simply identical), is one of the traits or tendencies that I find exemplified in a certain kind of 'theatricality'. Not necessarily in 'theatre', and not necessarily in everything that one would call 'theatrical', but in the questions and problems, challenges and injunctions that distinguish the history of 'theatricality' – if one can speak of such a history in the singular. One of the things that has struck me, in rethinking this history, at any rate certain parts of it, is the link between 'iterability', in English at least, and various forms of the present participle, including the 'gerund'. It is as if the conjugation of possibility with impossibility can be exemplified in what we call 'acting', as distinct from 'action', 'act' or 'actual(ity)': acting lacks the kind of reality usually associated with the present indicative, and yet it is bound up with 'indication' – although it is one that is never simply 'present' inasmuch as it is repetitive. At the same time, its 'repetition' is a rehearsal that is directed not just towards the past but above all towards the future – which, however, it will never fully 'attain' (that is, render present, actualize). This is why it is important to distinguish such iterative theatricality from 'performance' and 'performative', which often (if not always) imply the realization of an intention, of a purpose.

Understood in this way, you can see how such theatricalization could be situated in a series going back as far, at least, as Kant's definition of the beautiful as 'purposiveness without purpose'. The aesthetic judgement of beauty is addressed at something that is so immediately present that it can never be self-present, never identified. It remains purely indicative, a pointing-towards, a *Zweckmässigkeit ohne Zweck*. But this 'pointing towards' turns out, in Kant at any rate, to be even more a 'pointing away' – away from wherever it is at, and what it seems to be. Kant tries to synthesize this double movement in his notion of 'reflective judgement', but the notion only reproduces the split, since it designates a reflexivity that never arrives at its destination: a reflexivity without reflection, one could say, although I'm not at all sure that Kant would have been very happy with that formulation. But if one reads the Third Critique closely, one discovers that what Kant is describing, or rather trying to describe, is not a self-contained state but rather closer to the unstable aporia of a unity so self-contained that it tends to dissolve before our very eyes. This is why the 'as if' has to intervene so constantly, indeed so obsessively in that text, creating one parenthetic qualification after another, as Kant literally (or rather syntactically) ties himself into knots trying to articulate something according to a logic of identity it tends to undo. Kant's account of the aesthetic judgement of taste is a latter-day version of another of Nietzsche's favourite anecdotes: that of Cratylus outdoing his teacher, Heraclitus, when he notes that one cannot step into the same river 'even once'. Only Kant doesn't think that he is telling stories ... or does he?

I haven't touched on the 'technical' part of your question. Let me just say that the presentation of iterability that distinguishes theatrical 'representation' puts a particular spin on the question of 'technics'. If one remembers the earliest, pre-Heideggerian definitions of *techné* as involving a prosthetic supplement of an internal lack, then theatrical iterability locates that 'lack' in and as the 'act' of an 'actuality' that must be repeatable in order to be enacted. The 'en-' of 'enactment' is thus inseparable from the 'ex-' of an iterability that can never be self-contained. 'Theatricality' is what results when the impossibility of self-containment is exposed by iterability as a scene which is inevitably a 'stage', but which, as such, is determined by that which surrounds it, by what we call a 'theatre'. More affirmatively formulated, the impossibility of closure opens the scene to a space of alterity that is always provisionally embodied in and, even more, exposed as an 'audience' – singular noun for an irreducibly heteroclite stand-in. The 'audience' stands in for the others, those who were and those who will be – and perhaps even more, for those who will never come to be. Of course, it is in the nature of our socio-economic system, in an age of 'globalization', to do everything possible to appropriate and domesticate such 'standing-in' so that it seeks to fulfil itself in and as actual consumption.

The audience is thus considered by the commercial media predominantly, if not exclusively, as potential consumers.

Simon Morgan Wortham and Gary Hall (10 September 2001)

Presumably, then, the 'age of globalization' – as your work itself would indicate, and as you've perhaps hinted just now – is not and cannot be merely opposed to the issue and effects of 'theatricality', in which case the problem of, for want of a better term, the parergon which seems to re-emerge in the description you've just given of theatricalized space would also impose itself in any analysis of the globalized, technological age of today?

Samuel Weber (12 September 2001)

From the point of view I have begun to outline, 'theatricality' can provide a particularly interesting way of approaching 'globalization'. If one thinks about the word itself: the notion of the world as 'globe' suggests two things. First, something visible. Second, as a sphere, something self-contained. A 'world' is not necessarily visible: a 'globe' is, at least potentially. It is a visible *Gestalt*. As such, it implies a viewer. But this is no ordinary 'globe': it is, as just mentioned, a globe that contains everything. It is planetary, the site of all life as we know it, and in particular, of all human life. 'Globalization' in this sense implies totality (although not, in the literal sense, 'universality'): it defines the space or site of all options open to life in general, and to human life in particular. As a sphere, it is self-contained, even if it is not all-inclusive. Self-contained also suggests self-sufficient: the globe is the site of a life that can, and must, take care of itself.

And yet, as a visible *Gestalt*, anything that is 'global' is also an object of perception and of understanding. An object of consciousness and of cognition. But as the site of all life as we know it – and it is hardly an accident that 'globalization' coexists with, and perhaps encourages, a heightened fascination with the 'extraterrestrial' – 'globalization' names not so much an object as the conditions for all objectification, the conditions of cognition and of action. This is why we speak of 'globalization' and not just of the 'globe' or the 'global'. 'Global war', for instance, is a term that antedates the age of 'globalization'. 'Globalization' is a process by which the world of possibilities is at the same time totalized and restricted. This is why it serves as an appropriate figure to name a certain vision of the world in the post-Cold War period. The term 'globalization' does not merely emphasize the transnational interdependence of different parts of the world: it implies that there is no longer any alternative to the not-so-new world order of 'late' capitalism, and to the relations of power and hierarchies of subjugation that this order entails.

It implies this in a message that may often be transmitted subliminally, but that seeks to eliminate all ambiguity. Nevertheless, 'globalization' remains highly ambiguous, as a term and as a process, not so much in its message as in its means of address. For 'globalization' does not merely name a world-wide, socio-economic process: it also constitutes an address and an injunction, one that demands a response, which can vary between enthusiastic acceptance, and passionate rejection. Or also, resigned indifference, since the primary message conveyed by the word is that there can be no alternative except 'fanaticism', 'terrorism', and other forms of brutal irrationality. Globalization, as embodied in 'the media' – television above all, but also to a large extent in the print media – is presented as the only game in town, or rather, in the world. And this message is reinforced by the very existence and manifestation of media which themselves are part and parcel of its structure. Since there is ostensibly no alternative to 'globalization', in a world where ostentation and media are inseparable, the only response reserved for the audience is that of fundamental acquiescence, if not legitimation, in relation to the process, which in any case is presented as inevitable. Nevertheless, the media require this response in order that the process, which claims to be total and yet self-contained, can find its enabling limit. That limit is the acquiescence of the audience, by which the other, and alterity, is placed in the position of the consumer. Everything that globalization is not and cannot be is thus concentrated in and as its audience, which it produces as the limit that a capitalism-without-alternative strives both to produce and to appropriate.

In Derridean terms, one might say that the problem of the 'parergon' returns today in the form of the theatricalized audience: does it 'belong' to the 'work' as its intrinsic other, the way the consumer belongs to the process of production as its inner edge? Or does it split and dislocate such a dialectic by relating that which it delimits to what is irreducibly other? Or does it do both, and if so, in what proportions?

To take a horrific instance, one that is all too current at the time we are discussing this, but which will have become a more distant memory by the time our discussion reaches its 'audience', or rather readers: Yesterday, 11 September 2001, was the day on which the World Trade Centre was destroyed and the Pentagon badly damaged by what is called, understandably, a 'terrorist' attack. The destruction was transmitted, 'in real time', by television throughout the world, provoking, in the 'West', reactions of horror, and in parts of the Near

East (and perhaps elsewhere), spontaneous expressions of joy. These two very different responses seem to have nothing in common. And yet they share at least one interpretation of the destruction, which was presumably at the core both of the horror and of the joy: the discovery that no place on the globe could any longer consider itself safe, which is to say, immune to the violent effects of 'globalization'. Among the images of the destruction which returned incessantly on the television screen, one seemed to sum up one of the lessons of the horror: a plaque which was all that was left of one of the destroyed buildings, upon which was written: 'One World Centre'. And among the countless associations provoked by this remaining inscription, one that occurred to me, was that in today's 'One World', the 'Centre' was no longer safe from the 'periphery'. The sight of the two enormous towers not just collapsing, but imploding and disappearing into themselves, producing a huge cloud of dust and rubble, racing towards the camera, and, implicitly, towards the millions of viewers all over the world who sat in disbelief riveted to their screens – all of this exposed the 'One World Centre' to be as vulnerable as the peripheries. Was I the only viewer who was reminded of the chilling television depiction of 'The Day After', the white dust which coated everything in the 'nuclear winter' that followed a nuclear war between West and East? Was I the only one for whom the billowing clouds that rose from the collapsing towers recalled the mushroom clouds of previous nuclear explosions? And who then had to acknowledge that the spectacular destruction of 11 September was the result not of a high-tech explosion, but of a low-tech collision – one that was clearly highly organized and carefully planned, and executed with military precision, but apparently with the technology of the 'periphery', rather than that of the Centre.

From this standpoint, at least, 11 September has revealed the vulnerability of the most powerful political and economic structures, both in the literal and figurative sense. And in doing this it marks the end of an illusion – that of a *locus amoenus* existing at the Centre of the world-system. But at the same time, the bad tidings of this revelation are probably also experienced by many as a confirmation of their most deeply rooted fears, as well as a confirmation of the sense of powerlessness which is also one of the primary conditions of docile spectatordom.

The notion of 'theatricalization' includes this possibility – that of the docile, reactive, passive and anxious 'beholder' – but it can also reinscribe it in a space that exceeds the frame of spectacle and spectator. The danger is that such 'excess' will be experienced only as a source of anxiety and panic, and will thus be rejected and foreclosed by the kind of paranoiac spiral that words such as 'terrorism' and 'fanaticism' are designed to justify and promote.

Simon Morgan Wortham and Gary Hall (15 September 2001)

An initial reaction concerning what you've just said about recent events in the United States would be that the value of your remarks *at this time*[1] is certain, even if, as you seem to hint, they are bound inevitably to become an historical artefact: in a sense, a part, however small, of the 'events' themselves. And this, in turn, might prompt us to wonder about the complicated processes or relationships of partaking, participation and apartness upon which such a response – perhaps any sort of response – to these 'events' inevitably rests. Of course, the terms being used here deliberately recall, recite or replay key themes and issues within your own work, not least with regard to a whole range of questions having to do with criticism, spectatorship, viewpoint or standpoint, knowledge, judgement and so on. These questions install themselves, one might say, in philosophy and aesthetics, in literary, cultural and media studies, but also in the realms of politics, technologization and globalization.

Of course, some might find such reflections, or rather such self-reflexivity concerning the place or standpoint of any such critical response, to move in a direction that becomes rather self-regarding and, ultimately, a bit detached. On the other hand, by invoking the unstable dynamics of participation and apartness, as part of an appeal or injunction which in turn raises once more the question of parergon, limit, boundary or frame, such concerns could surely be viewed as entirely inseparable from what is most pressing among current international, political issues. And here again, in the very determination of the value or import of the question, the ambivalent interplay of apartness and participation imposes itself once more.

That said, it is also striking that there would seem to be a – perhaps uncanny – link between the question with which we began, concerning the uncanny, the response on your part, and subsequent events that have interrupted or imposed themselves upon this discussion. For instance, there is, in the first place, your awareness that what occurred on 11 September 2001 'will have become a more distant memory by the time our discussion reaches its "audience", or rather readers' – presumably because this is what has happened to similar events in the past. Immediate responses soon become reconsidered, mediated, over-written, transformed. There are already claims on the Net that the images which you refer to, of people in the Near East celebrating the attacks on the US, are in fact from old CNN footage dating from 1991.[1] On top of which is the fact that the events themselves resembled the 'theatrical' spectacles provided by any number of American films (*Independence Day*, *Mars Attacks*, which themselves link to the 'heightened fascination with the "extraterrestrial"' you speak of) – and one might note reports in the press that the release dates of a number of forthcoming films have been cancelled or postponed due to such similarities (Arnold Schwarzenegger's *Collateral Damage*, for example, which contains scenes of a building in LA being blown up, *Swordfish*, which has a city block being bombed, or *Big Trouble*, which involves a bomb on a plane). All this seems to add up to an uncanny sense, even when watching the events live on 11 September and being acutely aware of their singularity, that we have been here before; that we are being haunted by a certain repetition which is both 'always the same' and 'yet never entirely appropriable' – presenting us with a 'challenge' to which we have, as you have said, 'little choice but to respond'.

Samuel Weber (16 September 2001)

Let me respond, first, to the end of your comment, about the deprogramming of Hollywood catastrophe films, either new ones scheduled to come out in the near future, or older ones, which were to be shown on television (several such films will not be shown in the coming weeks as planned on French television). Although I assume that such deprogramming is a fairly general phenomenon, there is perhaps an additional development here in France that is equally significant. The week or so before the destruction of the World Trade Centre and the attack on the Pentagon, television viewers in France were treated to a rather unusual advertisement. It showed a worker cleaning the window of a skyscraper, when suddenly a glaring light coming from a mirror far below, in the street, blinds him but also the viewers themselves. Then, the worker loses his balance, and falls to certain death. But instead of striking the pavement, his body miraculously hits the roof of a car, a French car traditionally known for the spongy comfort of its suspension. The worker is saved.

On 11 September, that ad disappeared, presumably forever, from television and cinema screens. It was replaced by the sight of other bodies, this time 'real ones', falling to their death from far greater heights. One of the effects of this, expected and feared, is a very different kind of 'fall' tomorrow, when the American stock exchanges open, for the first time in almost a week. 'Consumer confidence', already badly shaken, is expected to be not the least significant of the 'collateral damage' caused by the attacks. But was not at least one of the underlying conditions of this 'catastrophe' already 'mirrored', as it were, in the ad that ran during the week preceding the attacks? If only the miraculous presence of the automobile below 'saved' the falling body from the fate visited upon the thousands caught in the upper stories of the two towers of the World Trade Centre Towers on 11 September, what can be said about 'the fear of falling' to which the advertisement appealed, just prior to the catastrophe? This ad, like all good advertising, struck a chord, was attuned to the expectations of its audience, even and especially those that are not necessarily conscious or avowed. For instance, the danger that provoked ('triggered') the fall of the window-washer also affected the spectators watching it: they, like he, were momentarily blinded by the glare. Where did the glare come from? Watching that ad, one could hardly avoid thinking of a deliberate, malicious, malevolent act: someone manipulating a mirror in order to blind the victim. But the 'victim' who is blinded also includes the beholder of the ad, to whom it is addressed. This puts the spectators, as potential consumers, in an 'analogous' position to the victim, who is saved by the potential object of consumption, the car.

The spectators watching the ad are, of course, the 'commodity' that commercial television sells to its clients, the advertisers. Their sight, and hence their status as spectators, are both 'struck' by the same glare that causes the 'worker' – the 'sight' they are given to see – to fall to an almost certain death. Only the automobile, a specific, distinct automobile, 'saves' the worker. By implication – however 'ironic' and even silly it may seem – only consumption of the commodity in question can 'save' the spectator. 'Datsun Saves!' From what? From the Fall, which, in the tradition of the religions of the Book, at least, means guilt and death.

This is not the place to develop the links between commodity consumption, on the one hand, and the notion of salvation on the other. It may therefore suffice to note that, in both, what is at stake is guilt on the one hand, and survival on the other. And not just survival, but survival of an individual who, otherwise, qua individual, is condemned to perish. This is also what links the ad I have just discussed to the Hollywood catastrophe films to which you refer, in which, almost always, the threat of disaster is averted or surmounted by the action of a single heroic individual. Individuals, as a 'class', category or collective, are vulnerable to 'terrorists', and only a heroic individual or, less frequently, a small group of individuals, can 'save' them. The action of an isolated individual redeems individual passivity and vulnerability, in the Hollywood scenarios at least.

That scenario is above all what 11 September has rendered obsolete. No Bruce Willis, Arnold Schwarzenegger or Harrison Ford could 'save' that day. Whether active or passive, the main role assigned to individuals on that day was that of perishing, or running from a danger that could hardly be circumscribed, much less effectively countered: billowing clouds of white smoke sowing panic before their advance (towards the cameras ...). And the main role assigned to the political embodiment of that sort of individualism was confusion and flight, symbolized by a President of the United States who is warned not to return 'home' but instead 'flies' – or rather, is flown – from military base to military base, in an effort to avoid the invisible dangers.

The spectre of invisibility persists in the aftermath of the attacks. All major figures of the American government, together with British Prime Minister Tony Blair, insist that a 'war' has broken out. But this war is haunted by enemies who, in the words of President Bush, 'believe they are invisible. Yet they are mistaken. They will be exposed and they will discover what others in the past have learned: Those who make war against the United States have chosen their own destruction' (Radio Address, 15 September 2001).

However, such enemies must first be located in order to be destroyed. And in order to be located, they must be 'seen'. With astonishing rapidity, an automobile is found with the Koran, flight manuals, maps and other unmistakable indications. Within two days, pictures and names of the hijackers are flashed across the screens, their whereabouts and histories described in detail. But the direct perpetrators themselves can no longer be seized, much less punished. All the more important, then, to be able to name and depict – that is, see – and thus to call to account the mastermind of the destruction. The importance attached to the figure of the individual – above all, to the face, but also to the body once again, as previously in the Gulf War – culminates in the identification of a new, Satanic (Islamic) Anti-Christ. Within hours of the attacks, the bearded figure of Osama bin Laden appears on television and computer screens throughout the world as 'prime suspect'. Somewhat less prominence is given to his writings, with the notable exception of the *fatwa* of 1998, signed by Osama bin Laden but also by a number of other persons, proclaiming that: 'The ruling to kill the Americans and their allies – civilians and military – is an individual duty for every Muslim who can do it in any country in which it is possible to do it'. This phrase is quoted again and again, without any indication that it is part of a larger statement, the remainder of which is almost never cited: ' . . . in order to liberate the al-Aqsa Mosque and the holy mosque [Mecca] from their grip, and in order for their armies to move out of all the lands of Islam, defeated and unable to threaten any Muslim.' The amputation of the arguments upon which the *fatwa* is based, as well as the focus on a single individual or group, provides the groundwork for the preparation of the Crusade against the Anti-Christ, if not for the War of Civilizations between the Judaeo-Christian and Moslem worlds long prophesized by Samuel Huntington.

The notion of a 'War of Civilization' – or rather, of Civilization against the Barbarians – strives to promote the sense of 'distance' between friend and enemy so necessary to the detached positioning of the omniscient and secure observer. It also prepares those observers to embrace a solution of the conflict through military intervention. What you refer to as 'participation' is acknowledged, but few consequences are drawn from it that might disturb this 'friend–enemy' dichotomy. The fact that Western governments, and in particular the UK and US, have historically sought to defend their interests in the Arab world by supporting authoritarian and often conservative, theological and political forms of Islam – the Saudi Arabian Wahhabi Islam is probably the most visible instance, but by no means the only one – while often, and concomitantly, weakening secular political governments and groups – is, of course, 'acknowledged' but also 'isolated', in the Freudian sense, which is to say, cut off from its consequences, the most terrible of which we have just experienced, but whose consequences may prove to be even more destructive.

This is just one crass instance of how the systematic denial of 'participation' in the name of a Manichean dualism of friend and enemy can contribute to the dangerous situation in which we now find ourselves. The same forces that participated in fostering the conditions and promoting the rise of 'Islamic Fundamentalism' are now obliged to destroy those parts of it that have escaped their control. An old story, but with new and terrifying consequences, since the 'Centre' can no longer take for granted that it will be protected from the events of 'the periphery'. And it is likely that this all too justified fear will now be exploited to strengthen the very forces and situations that brought it about in the first place.

Simon Morgan Wortham and Gary Hall (17 September 2001)

With regard to events of 'the periphery' returning to haunt the 'Centre', and concerning also the idea of decentred networks of opposition which are often hard to locate and see, we might come back, a little differently perhaps, to the issue of 'globalization'. What do you make of a different form of asymmetrical attack on the 'West': what might be said of the anti-globalization protestors (of Seattle, Prague, Genoa, the anti-sweatshop campaigns directed at the likes of Gap by some students in some universities in the US, and so forth)? In particular, how do these protestors fit into your analysis of American liberal society, for example in *Institution and Interpretation*? One thinks specifically of the chapter on 'Capitalizing History', which includes an analysis that is based on a reading of Hartz's *The Liberal Tradition in America*. Are these 'protests' (one is wary of terming something so decentred a 'movement') just introducing conflict into a pluralist, non-conflictual space? Or is this space being revealed as conflictual by these protests? And if so, is there any extent to which this is a result or an effect of what, for shorthand, might be termed 'theory' (in its very broadest conceptualization) – despite and for all of Naomi Klein's indirect critique of the latter in her book *No Logo* – given that it was 'theory' which 'relegitimized' such 'conflict', not just 'within' fields and institutions, but 'of' fields and institutions? Klein interestingly sees what she labels as 'identity politics', and with which she associates 'postmodern academics' and the 'theory' of Gayatri Spivak, as the immediate precursor of the anti-globalization protestors: it is against such 'identity politics' that the current generation is in part reacting, apparently. Klein is thus just one of those who have recently chastized 'theory' (among other things) for 'not being political enough', in favour of a concern for the 'real', the material and the economic. But isn't the idea precisely of a reaction to 'theory', as well as the notion of theory relegitimizing a certain kind of conflict, bound to create problems for this kind of approach?

Samuel Weber (17 September 2001)

To create a bridge from our previous discussion to your questions, an article in today's *International Herald Tribune* describes al-Qa'ida (the 'Base'), the organization founded by Osama bin Laden and accused by US authorities of being responsible for last week's attacks, as an 'example of globalization' (Karen DeYoung and Michael Dobbs, *IHT*, 17 September 2001). The comparison could be illuminating. What the authors have in mind is not just the international scope of the organization, but its mode of operation, the relation of the individual, relatively autonomous groups, operating all over the world, to the chain of command, its 'base', presumably situated in the Middle East and very likely in Afghanistan. The very notion of 'base' seems to change, given that it seems to include alliances of different sorts (tactical, strategic) with other groups, not directly linked to Osama bin Laden. The notion of 'globalization' is thus associated not just with world-wide reach, but with an organizational structure in which the relation of 'parts' to 'whole' is very different from traditional 'organic' structures, be they of a traditional military sort, or a traditional political–conspiratorial sort (that is, the 'democratic centralism' of revolutionary Communist parties). Such a transformed structure, which permits what is probably an even greater autonomy to the individual units than in conspiratorial groups of the past, is probably itself a response to the changed needs of such groups, faced with the technology of globalization and the new means of surveillance and repression it has developed. Such surveillance is epitomized on the one hand by the spy satellites that are capable literally of surveying the 'globe', and on the other hand by the network 'Echelon' based mainly in the Anglophone countries of the world: the US, Great Britain, Australia, New Zealand and their possessions.

But the comparison becomes truly suggestive when, against this background of commonality, one begins to discern some of the differences between the global quality of an organization such as al-Qa'ida and what is generally understood, and practised, as 'globalization'. Not for nothing was the prime target in the attacks of the past weeks two buildings known as 'The World Trade Centre'. As I already have suggested, the 'fundamentalists' are not quite as 'fundamental' as this label might suggest. They targeted, and destroyed, the symbol of World Trade: that is, not just of Globalization, and not just of American or Western or of Judaeo-Christian Civilization, but of World Finance Capitalism. This is a point that is being studiously obscured in the American media, although obviously it cannot be entirely ignored. However, there is a rather quick generalization that takes place in this discourse, in which 'finance' and 'trade' are replaced by 'freedom' and 'civilization', in order to portray the attackers as 'fanatics' and 'fundamentalists'.

To strike at the World Trade Centre, and then at the Pentagon (with either the White House or the Capitol as the third intended target) is thus to use certain aspects of 'globalization' – the dispersed, decentred, portable and transportable aspects of its technology – against the primary aim of globalization as it dominates the world today, which is the extraction and appropriation of profit through the production and circulation of commodities. The 'religious' programme to expel Western infidels from the holy areas of Islam is inseparable from a socio-economic situation caused by a historically specific political relation of forces.[2]

The symbolic significance of the attack on the symbol of global finance, the World Trade Centre, together with the symbol of the state institution that maintains the present relation of forces throughout the world, namely, the Pentagon – all of this is, in the words of a French specialist on international law, Professor Brigitte Klein, 'breathtaking' in its precision. It is 'real' and 'symbolic', and the 'symbolic' element contributes and adds to the 'real'.

So if the attacks on these symbols were made possible by an organization that shared certain traits with 'globalization', and in this sense was indeed 'part' of it, they were also clearly intended to call attention to, and discredit, certain other aspects of the very same process. And yet, there is another constituent of this 'action' that clearly distinguishes it from the capitalist mainstream of globalization. It is what is referred to, not accidentally, as its 'kamikaze' element: the readiness to give one's life to accomplish one's goal. This is a dimension which, unless I am sorely mistaken, is fundamentally missing from what might be called the mainstream 'culture' of globalization, inasmuch at least as the dominant aim of that culture – that which determines the primary directions in which it moves – is that of the private appropriation of profit and the increased level of consumption which that appropriation makes possible. This is the point where what has been called a 'war of civilizations' may not be an entirely ideological phrase – although it is clearly one that is being used to obscure more than to enlighten.

Let me illustrate what I have in mind by pointing to another ad, this time a full-page ad published in the 13 September issue of the *International Herald Tribune* (and doubtless elsewhere as well). The entire background of the page is blue-grey, 75 per cent is sky, 25 per cent is frozen tundra. On what appears to be the frozen surface of a lake, not far from one of the poles, three tiny figures can be seen, two children and one adult. One of the tiny child-figures appears to be bent forward, skating or skiing perhaps, in any event poised for something, balancing. S/he is observed, a few feet away, by an adult. A second child is walking towards the two others from the side. High above this scene, two words stand out in large, white type: 'We're out.' Four inches lower, in much smaller white type, the message: 'Vodafone Voicemail. Get away from it all. Well, for an hour or two.' Further down still, the line: 'How are you?' And finally, not far from the three small figures, who are enclosed in a bubble, like those in which comic-strip characters speak, the message: 'The people you need are only a touch away.'

In the immediate aftermath of 11 September, nothing, of course, looks or is the same as it might have seemed before. The poignant appeals coming from the cell-phones of those trapped in the burning towers were cries of goodbye, of leave-taking from 'the people' who were 'only a touch away'. But did this touch fulfil the ad's promise: to 'get away from it all. Well, for an hour or two'? Scarcely an hour was granted those caught in the planes or the towers. Those who were able to get out of the towers may have survived, but none, it is fairly certain, will ever be able to 'get away from it all', not even 'for an hour or two'. And yet, this is precisely what the ad proclaims: 'We're out.' Who, we? The events of 11 September suggest that it is getting harder and harder 'to get out'.

Except perhaps for the hijackers themselves. Or the suicide bombers. They are, or will be, 'out' and 'away from it all' – but not just 'for an hour or two'. We want to 'get away from it all', 'get out', for an hour or two – but only before going back 'in', presumably refreshed. Those who perpetrate such attacks are ready to go 'out' without coming back. Perhaps because they were never 'in', or at any rate couldn't stay in. This difference is perhaps one reason why the horrific vision of the towers collapsing inwards into themselves, imploding rather than exploding, is so haunting: the nightmare vision of an immanence disappearing into itself. The attacks were also against the kind of secular 'immanence' that those towers both represented and also implemented.

This is, of course, a very different rejection from that which led protestors to the streets of Seattle, Prague and Genoa. Like the conspirators, these protestors were also 'decentred' but at the same time for the most part not organized in secret organizations and obviously in their majority with very different aims. These were informed by notions such as 'sustainability of resources' and other 'ecological' considerations, as well as the more traditional political values of social and economic justice. Beyond that, given the heterogeneity of the different components participating in the protests, it would be precipitous to relate them to the kind of analysis I sketched out in 'Capitalizing History', since we are doubtless dealing with considerable diversity, and hence, with very different political and moral perspectives. For instance, the differences among the different 'Green' movements, their similarities and divergences with respect to the group 'ATTAC', comprise a vast spectrum of opposition to the reigning form of globalization (but not necessarily to all of its aspects, as ATTAC constantly insists). Some of this opposition could no doubt be shown to depend upon the kinds of 'naturalizing' that Hartz attributes to the American liberal tradition – but certainly not all of it. It is not, after all, a uniquely American phenomenon. Much would depend upon the way in which these different protests articulate or define their relation to the 'future'. But this would require very minute and detailed analyses, which I can't even begin to attempt here.

As to the 'chastizing' of 'theory' for not being 'political enough', it's an all too familiar 'logo'; an easy enough exercise especially if one limits oneself to pointing at the distance that separates thinking, of whatever kind, and 'action', which is usually considered the *sine qua non* of the 'political'. But to do this in the name of something called 'the real', 'the material' or even 'the economic' (and it should be obvious that I much prefer the latter to the former), can also open the door to the worst kind of dogmatism. If 'the real' is what resists, or, as Freud writes about 'reality testing', what returns, remains, then access to it will always be immensely difficult, complex and never entirely attainable. Conceptual formations such as 'the real', which claim both singularity and generality, can even become pernicious when they claim, explicitly or implicitly, to bridge the gap between the two. Suspicion directed at conceptual generality is one of the leitmotifs of modern thought, going back at least to the Scholastics, and the struggle of Nominalists against Realists. This assumes a distinctly contemporary cast with the critique of Hegel by Kierkegaard and Marx. Critique, of course, is never enough, and if 'theory' means the self-contained study of theoretical utterances, then it should be 'criticized'. But clearly this is not what most thinkers identified with critical and deconstructive thought of the past decades have done. Almost all have been concerned with the political dimensions, consequences and conditions of their thinking, and of their writing, and the shift from the one to the other is precisely an articulation of this concern. What I have tried to develop concerning the theatrical dimension of inscription, of its propagation and transformation, is an attempt to elaborate this dimension.

It is perhaps worth recalling that there is a difference in being 'political' at the level of propositional statements (that is, making declarations, signing petitions and so on) and being political at the level of the established codes of articulation to which one is necessarily submitted, but which are also susceptible to change. This is why a certain thinking of virtuality, possibility, potentiality – what in a study of Benjamin I call his '-abilities', a certain virtualization of conceptualization itself, of 'meaning' – can be politically effective, even if it never gets its act together. This doesn't dispense with more conventional forms of 'political' analysis and interpretation, much less with 'political action', but it does affect, and possibly transform, the grids within which such actions and interpretations have to be situated.

Simon Morgan Wortham and Gary Hall (18 September 2001)

It is interesting that you draw to a close the comment you've just made by saying 'there is a difference in being "political" at the level of propositional statements (that is, making declarations, signing petitions, and so on) and being political at the level of the established codes of articulation to which one is necessarily submitted, but which are also susceptible to change'. Presumably, this statement could be taken to re-mark at least one of the borders or crossroads in our discussion so far. It could be seen as installing itself in or as one of the places where we find ourselves situated between problems and questions that are ostensibly 'philosophical' or 'theoretical' in nature, and others that are normally designated as 'political'. Doubtless our exchange has tried to trace, and even assume, the very complex traits that tangle or tear together the conflictually riven territory of these supposedly different concerns, 'fields' or 'disciplines'. It is in this context that we'd risk introducing – in however jarring a way – a question we'd been thinking of asking you beforehand, to see whether it is as far removed as it might seem from the question of 'politics' – and, indeed, from the politics of 'theatricalization', of 'propositional statements' and of 'codes of articulation'.

　　In your recent work on theatricality as medium, much of it as yet unpublished, you comment on the way in which the writing of Jacques Derrida explores its own 'theatrical' quality as a 'staging'. But what of the performance or performativity that attends your own writing? What of its own 'taking place'? Does this open up or open on to a different sort of 'theatrical/theoretical' space or (dis-)location? While it can be argued that the tracing out of certain effects of iterability or performativity in – and between – your texts is an indispensable element in the reading of them, some might say that, unlike the Derridean texts which you perhaps tend to privilege in your work (in the more recent material on theatricality, it's Derrida's 'The Double Session', while elsewhere, at the end of *Institution and Interpretation*, it's his 'Envois') you yourself don't seem to 'theatrically stage' the texts you write about. At least, not quite so explicitly. That is, you don't seem to perform or act them out in quite the same way that, say, Derrida does with Mallarmé. Rather, you might appear, to some readers, to remain uncannily the same throughout much of your writing. But do you stop short of retaining your own authorial identity throughout, and, if so, how? For example, would the uncanny experience of the 'familiar' in your writing in fact involve a certain theatricalization, in that we find there (to borrow your own words): 'not the communication of something new in the sense of content, but the variation of something familiar through its repetition'? Is your very recognizable style – if we might call it that – the effect of a deliberate strategy on your part? Or is it, as you say in *Mass Mediauras*, in response to a question on the 'clarity' of your writing, the result, not of 'making or taking decisions but of being taken – even overtaken! – by them' (CU, 195)?

This, at any rate, was the question we had in mind. Not for the first time in our discussion, such questions or issues risk seeming quite remote from – and even discontinuous with – the current events with which we are all preoccupied. At first glance, they seem to stand apart and refuse to participate. But the last part of your previous set of remarks, on theatricality and on action and articulation in particular, would seem to allow such concerns to partake of the 'political' which otherwise might exclude them. For instance, would you be able, at this time, to reflect further on the (political?) relationship, if there is any, between the kind of acts or 'events' with which we are very much concerned now, today, and the kind of act we are engaged in, now, over a number of days, this discussion taking place?

Another, perhaps related, question that we'd send you at the same time and, once more, concerning 'politics' – assuming we can even begin to know what that term means today. The emphasis on institutions and instituting in your work has been presented as a way of making deconstruction 'political'. (Godzich offers a reading along these lines in his 'Afterword' to *Institution and Interpretation*.) And, indeed, you yourself have argued (in 'The Limits of Professionalism') that deconstruction, in what you call 'its orthodox form', downplays the forces and powers that maintain certain sets of paradigms, certain authorities and systems. But doesn't this reading (of both your work and deconstruction) rather imply: (a) that other 'deconstructions' – those that are not concerned with questions of the institution and instituting, force and power – are not political; and (b) that the question of the political is decided in advance – this constituting a limiting of the political, an acceptance of the political as it is institutionally defined, of the sort you elsewhere argue against? In addition, does the supposed affiliation between 'instituting', 'institutions' and 'the political' as outlined above – and, indeed, the decision as to what these terms mean –

need to be rethought in light of some of the effects of 'globalization' witnessed in the events of the past week?

Samuel Weber (18 September 2001)

Both of your questions presuppose a consensual understanding of just what is meant by 'political'. Underpinning such an understanding, I see further questions: Is the political necessarily tied to the state? To society? Is it primarily a question of Power? Of the Common Good? The General Will? Community? Is it manifest primarily in 'action'? In strategies? In policies? Is it necessarily bound up with 'subjects', in either the philosophical, grammatical or social sense of the word? What is its relation to spatial and temporal factors: to the organization of space through the assigning of places, and to the organization of time through the regulation of past, present and future?

Take, once again, the events of 11 September. I call them 'events' because this word seems best to condense and to complicate the two meanings of the term with which I am familiar: first, the usual use of the term in English, to designate a spatio-temporally localizable occurrence; and, second, the Heideggerian meaning of *Ereignis*, designating an unpredictable, uncontrollable outbreak that disrupts spatial and temporal continuities and dislocates and transforms frames of reference. What happened on 11 September was an event in both senses. It involved the destruction of specific buildings and the more or less immediate after-effects of that destruction, all of which can and was represented in unforgettable images that will haunt most of us for many years to come. And at the same time, these events also involved a far less visible network, not intangible, but this time more difficult to localize – the problem of the American 'response' – and thus to reduce to a single, identifiable object or set of objects. Organizationally there is 'the base', but it is at the same time a kind of 'superstructure'. Or rather, sub- and infrastructure. The 'base' is not identical with those structures, but is also not simply their foundation. That is the problem of the 'war' or 'crusade' against 'terrorism': finding the proper target or targets. Colin Powell and others have compared Osama bin Laden's organization to a 'holding'; others, to a 'multinational' – but those terms serve more to describe the perspective of those who use them than the very different situation of their adversaries.

Were the events of 11 September 'political'? Did they involve 'politics'? Much of the official discourse of the American government, and much (although certainly not all) of American media, tends to deny this, at least implicitly. According to this perspective, 11 September was the work of religious fanatics, of resentment, of 'evil' in its purest form. It is to be combated morally, in a 'crusade' (President Bush) that will extirpate its perpetrators. At the same time, the same discourse insists on the term 'war' to describe what has happened, as well as the proper response to it. 'America's New War' is CNN's heading or title for Chapter Two of its 'story'. 'War' is generally considered a 'political' phenomenon, but is a 'crusade' a 'war'? It is true that the two words have been used as equivalents in American discourse of the past few decades: 'War against Drugs', 'War against Poverty', 'War against Crime' and, today, 'War against Terrorism'. But such a use employs the word to designate a general mobilization of a nation against an enemy that is not necessarily identifiable with a state, and hence which is not 'political' in the most familiar sense of this word.

The problem in doing 'justice' to 'the political' is the 'cut' required to define the term. 'State', 'power', 'action' – the triad presupposed in most consensual definitions of the term – are notions that operate like 'freeze-frame photographs' (*Momentaufnahmen* as one says in German, literally, instantaneous), bringing to a halt an ongoing and highly complex and dynamic network of relations that is constantly evolving and therefore only provisionally delimitable. The dilemma of the American response to the attacks of 11 September illustrates this problem all too well. The 'culprits', like many of their victims, are dead. They therefore cannot be brought to justice, only identified, which was accomplished with a speed that is all the more surprising given the apparent lack of preparedness. At the same time, the problem of 'terrorism' cannot be limited to al-Qa'ida, Osama bin Laden or even to Muslim Fundamentalism, as the last great attack on American soil in Oklahoma City clearly demonstrated. But how then can it be sufficiently delimited to serve as a target of effective action? Are the roots of this 'terrorism' political? Religious? Economic? Cultural?

To be sure, the discourses of the media, and that of the American government, in no way exhaust the phenomenon of 'the political', but they do manifest certain widely held attitudes and conceptions that are by no means foreign to the Academy (at least in the US). Charlotte Raven, writing in the British *Guardian*, touched a nerve when she observed:

At the root of this (official discourse) is an overwhelming need to control meaning. America can't let the world speak for itself. It was taken unawares last Tuesday and part of the trauma of that event was the shock of being forced to listen to a message that it hadn't had time to translate. The subsequent roar of anger was, amongst other things, the sound of the US struggling to regain the right to control its own narrative. It did this by declaring war. By this means, Bush ensured that America only had to sit with the inexplicable for a couple of anxious days. After that, the sense, so unfamiliar to them, of not knowing what had happened or what it meant was replaced by the reassuring certainties of John Brown's body and calls for national unity. By turning what should have been a criminal manhunt into an all-out war, Bush was asserting his right to define America's reality. Instead of submitting to the reality, he created the situation he wanted, fashioning a plausible, beatable enemy. (*The Guardian*, 18 September 2001)

Translating the traumatic into the elements of an all too familiar narrative – Bush describing the 'justice' he seeks in terms of the Hollywood Western, 'Wanted, Dead or Alive' – condenses a certain conception of 'the political': the state, represented by the sheriff, leading the posse, locates the outlaw, neutralizes him, 'dead or alive' – and presumably collects the reward. Raven is correct, I believe, in emphasizing that a certain narrative is crucial for framing this conception. For only a certain form of narrative allows time and space to be subordinated to meaning as media of self-fulfilment rather than of self-destruction.

The belief that this self-contained narrative, consisting of a continuum of beginning, middle and end, providing the sole paradigm of meaning, reality and identity – a belief that is not limited to the practice or study of literature, but that rather sustains and informs the practices and institutions, the perceptual and conceptual grids of the very 'civilization' that erected the twin towers to celebrate, and concentrate, 'World Trade' – is as much, if not more, a part of 'politics' as is the triad of state, power and action that constitutes its most obvious and traditional manifestation.

It is the self-evidence, the self-contained 'reality' of this narrative scheme that is challenged, disrupted and dislocated by many, if not all, of what are called 'deconstructive' texts. Obviously, such dislocation operates in very different ways and to very different degrees. What I have called 'theatricalization' is one part of it: by foregrounding the 'stage', it resituates familiar narratives so that their framing function is no longer taken for granted. The 'scene' is what exceeds but also enables any single, self-contained narrative to take place. Such staging has become fairly evident in the later writings of Derrida, as it also did in the later writings of Lacan. But it can be operative without being as obvious or manifest. It is 'at work' wherever the expected, established expectations of readers (viewers, listeners) find themselves challenged and in some way forced to adjust, to move, to change. This is obviously a long way from what is generally recognized as effective 'political action'. But the determination of what is 'effective' is never a simple given, just as it is never a simple question of personal preference, never simply aleatory.

With respect to my own writing, it is certainly less 'theatrical' than that of either Lacan or Derrida, even if theatricality is more 'thematized', more explicitly discussed in my work. Perhaps one reason for the difference is that my writing is less rooted in a single discourse and tradition than is Derrida's or Lacan's, or Benjamin's for that matter. Certain major impulses have come to me precisely from the encounter of different cultures and languages: first, German, then French, both always interacting with a certain (American) English. Perhaps this is one reason why a certain 'intensity' did not develop in the way it has in Derrida's writing, an aspect he has described as his 'monolinguism'.

If you are asking about this kind of difference, then it is surely not simply a 'deliberate strategy' on my part, but something that my experience – trajectory – has imposed upon me. Which doesn't mean that it couldn't change in the future. But certainly that change will never be absolute: it will always be, I fear, more or less recognizable. But with luck, it will not just be 'more of the same'.

Perhaps this is why one of my next projects, which is already 'mired' in repetition, and in a certain sense is therefore anything but entirely 'new', involves a 'return' to the question of the uncanny, which I began studying some 35 years ago, but which only fairly recently I have tried to rethink in terms of a certain theatricality. It is curious that such a significant notion should have received so little attention over the past years. Derrida, once again, seems to be almost alone in his sustained concern for this strangely familiar topic. But even he has published relatively little sustained analysis of it so far, although he has discussed it at length in several of his unpublished seminars. My suspicion is that at least part of the explanation for this benign neglect has to do with the singularly elusive character of the uncanny: is it a concept, an experience, a feeling? Is it historically conditioned or transhistorical? At any rate, it seems profoundly linked to the end of an epoch obsessed with reflexivity and self-consciousness, while also announcing things to come in an as yet undecipherable language.

Simon Morgan Wortham and Gary Hall (20 September 2001)

A final question which, given its nature, you may feel unable to answer without referring once more to events of a contemporary nature. In 'Force of Law', Derrida names 'justice' as the one thing that cannot be deconstructed. In 'The Debts of Deconstruction' you seem to add to the list of things that cannot be deconstructed deconstruction's own debts, and furthermore the 'question of debt in general'. One might wonder where this leaves the question of your own relationship and debts to Derrida and to deconstruction? But, beyond this, what then becomes of the relationship of 'justice' to 'debt'? Is this of special relevance today?

Samuel Weber (21 September 2001)

One of the texts I discuss in 'The Debts of Deconstruction' was from Nietzsche's *Genealogy of Morals*, where he speculates that the stronger a group or 'tribe' becomes, the greater its sense of indebtedness to its antecedents. This in turn results in a 'fear' of 'forefathers' who have become 'divinely uncanny and unimaginable'. In the end, says Nietzsche, the fear produced by this sense of unrequitable debt transfigures the ancestor into a god. The origin of the gods, then, would 'perhaps' be this fear.

But such a birth of the gods out of fear is itself based on the presupposition of an originary equivalence, and therefore of a debt that is held to subvene upon a relation that would otherwise be balanced. It is this balance-sheet of identity, of commensurability, that Derrida's notion of 'justice' unbalances. The scales of this justice are not balanced, they are always already tipped, one way or the other, and indeed only thinkable from this situation of imbalance.

Nietzsche's account here profoundly modifies our usual conception of debt, and its relation to a debtor. We usually think of a debt as something that can and must be 'had': one 'has' a debt; it is assignable to a debtor. This debtor in turn is defined by this negative property, 'his' (or 'her') debt. But the debt, as Derrida negotiates it, is not just a debt to another (ego, self): it is that which indebts the self itself to the other. It is therefore never something that you can 'have', or that can be assigned to you in an unequivocal manner. It is both yours and not yours, part of you and that which parts with you, or rather, causes you to take leave from, and of, yourself.

There is a word, difficult if not impossible to translate into English, which Derrida uses to describe such a movement, in its irreducibility. In a very long footnote, running across several pages of *De l'esprit*, Derrida demonstrates that Heidegger's notion of thinking as questioning in turn presupposes something that Heidegger calls *Zuspruch* or *Zusage*, a kind of call or appeal, for which the closest nominal equivalent in English seems to be 'appeal' but which corresponds more closely, perhaps, with the idiomatic phrase 'speak to'. Thinking as questioning thus never constitutes an absolute beginning or origin, but rather responds to an appeal. This appeal, as it is formulated in German by Heidegger (based on the roots, *Spruch* and *Sage*), is inseparable from language, understood as a practice or movement, a heightened receptivity, an opening to the other, a disposition to listen, discern, respond, rather than as an entity or system – understood, in short, as a saying rather than as a statement or proposition. But at the same time it antedates, precedes the constitution and acquisition of language as a positive entity. And such a disposition, Derrida argues, involves not simply the assumption of a 'debt' but the giving of what he calls – and here we come to that untranslatable word – a *gage*. In English, we would probably have to translate this as a 'deposit', or possibly wager. The *gage* is thus both a sort of guarantee for the repayment of a debt and a gamble, a promise, an engagement. But there is a difference: the deposit is deposited somewhere, in a safe place. It is a form of placement. For Derrida, by contrast, the *gage* whose appeal precedes and permits all questioning, says 'yes', affirms, but without positing anything. It quite literally, but not idiomatically, de-posits. And it does so by responding to 'an event, the memory (*mémoire*) of which precedes all remembrance (*souvenir*) and to which we are bound by a faith that defies all narrative' (*De l'esprit*).

To be sure, Derrida here is reading, interpreting, Heidegger. But at the same time, on the margins of the main text, in this long footnote, he is also writing and commenting in the most literal sense – thinking with, which means also translating, re-marking, doing justice not to 'Heidegger' as author, philosopher or subject, but as a text that is anything but self-identical, harmonious or self-contained. Derrida's text engages Heidegger by doing justice not to the spirit but to the letters of his texts, by taking up their challenge, their '*gage*', without the security of an original, underlying or overriding meaning. By remarking Heidegger's assertion, that 'language must already appeal or have appealed to us' (*muss sich die Sprache zuvor uns zusagen oder gar schon zugesagt haben*) *De l'esprit* reshuffles the deck of our usual reading of Heidegger, and of much more, by foregrounding the condition of all engagement, political or other, as residing in a certain disposition to assume and respond to the *gage*. There must be a disposition to engage that presupposes every organization of space and time into places, objects and, above all, narratives, 'in' which one could place, or deposit, one's engagement. There must be an acceptance of 'faith' that antedates everything 'in' which one could have faith. The '*gage*' that doesn't secure is this faith that de-fies all narrative.

Another word for this faith is, perhaps, 'justice'. But not 'infinite justice' as the unending triumph of Good over Evil. This is precisely the kind of narrative that justice must 'de-fy'.

Today, more than ever, justice demands the de-fiance of all narratives, especially those that seem the most self-evident, the most compelling, and that are therefore perhaps the most dangerous.

Notes

1 This claim has since been retracted. The reference to the original claim on the web is: http://indymedia.org/front.php3?article_id = 63288&group = webcast. The retraction is at: http://www.indymedia.org/front.php3?article_id = 64366.

2   The remark of Professor Robert Precht is worth noting in his context. Professor
    Precht served as public defender of one of those accused in the 1993 bombing of the
    World Trade Centre. His conclusion about the state of mind and motivations of
    those involved in this attack can serve as a valuable warning against easy
    stereotypes. 'The things that struck me were the very complicated feelings the people
    who commit these acts have for America,' he said. 'Our leaders describe them as
    evildoers and say they hate everything our country stands for .... That was not my
    experience.' He said that several of the defendants admired the US system of
    government and law and had a real knowledge of American history. But they
    resented US policies. The dispute which terrorists have with America is really more a
    political one and has nothing to do with Islamic beliefs, Precht asserted. Instead, he
    declared, 'these are simply people who develop political agendas and then dress them
    up in a cloak of righteousness' (Kathy Barr Hoffmann, 'Attacks Remind Professor
    of 1993', *Associated Press*, 1 October 2001).

Bibliography of Selected Works in English by Samuel Weber

'The Madrepore', *MLN*, 87 (1972), 915–61.

'The Sideshow, Or, Remarks on a Canny Moment', *MLN*, 88 (1973), 1102–33.

'The Responsibility of the Critic: A Response', *MLN*, 91 (1976), 814–16.

'Saussure and the Apparition of Language: The Critical Perspective', *MLN*, 91 (1976), 913–38.

'The Divaricator: Remarks on Freud's *Witz*', *Glyph*, 1 (1977), 1–27.

'It', *Glyph*, 4 (1978), 1–31.

Unwrapping Balzac. A Reading of La Peau de Chagrin (Toronto: University of Toronto Press, 1979).

'Closure and Exclusion', Diacritics, 10:2 (1980), 35–46.

'Translating the Untranslatable': Introduction to Theodor Adorno's *Prisms*, trans. Samuel and Shierry Weber (Cambridge, MA: MIT Press, 1981), 9–15.

The Legend of Freud (Minneapolis: University of Minnesota Press, 1982).

'The Limits of Professionalism', *Oxford Literary Review*, 5:1–2 (1982), 59–74.

'A Stroke of Luck', *Enclitic*, 6:2 (1982), 29–31.

'The Critics' Choice', in Francis Barker *et al.* (ed.), *Reading, Writing, Revolution* (Colchester: Publications of the University of Essex, 1982), 147–58.

'Capitalising History: *The Political Unconscious*', *Diacritics*, 13:2 (1983), 14–28.

'Reading and Writing—*chez* Derrida', *Tijdschrift Voor Filosofie*, 45:1 (1983), 41–62.

'The Debts of Deconstruction and Other, Related Assumptions', in Joseph H. Smith and William Kerrigan (eds), *Taking Chances: Derrida, Psychoanalysis, and Literature* (Baltimore and London: Johns Hopkins University Press, 1984), 33–65.

'Taking Place: Toward a Theater of Dislocation', *Enclitic*, 8:1–2 (1984), 124–43, also in David J. Levin (ed.), *Opera Through Other Eyes* (Stanford, CA: Stanford University Press, 1993), 107–46.

'How Not to Stop Worrying', *Critical Exchange*, 15 (1984), 17–25.

'The Debt of Criticism: Notes on Stanley Fish's *Is There a Text in This Class?*', *Critical Exchange*, 15 (1984), 17–26.

'The Intersection: Marxism and the Philosophy of Language', *Diacritics* 15:4 (1985), 94–110.

'Literature – Just Making It', afterword to Jean-Francois Lyotard and Jean-Loup Thebaud, *Just Gaming*, trans. Wlad Godzich (Minneapolis: University of Minnesota Press, 1985), 101–20.

'Ambivalence: The Humanities and the Study of Literature', *Diacritics*, 15:2 (1985), 11–25.

'Introduction', *Glyph*, 1 (New Series) (1986), ix–xii.

'Caught in the Act of Reading', *Glyph*, 1 (New Series) (1986), 181–214.

'Laughing in the Meanwhile', *MLN*, 102 (1987), 691–706.

Institution and Interpretation (Minneapolis: University of Minnesota Press, 1987).

'The Foundering of Comparative Literature', in Clayton Koelb and Susan Noakes (eds), *Aspects of Comparative Literature* (Ithaca, NY: Cornell University Press, 1998), 57–72.

'Introduction', in D.P. Schreber, *Memoirs of my Nervous Illness* (Cambridge, MA: Harvard University Press, 1988), vii–liv.

'The Monument Disfigured', in Werner Hamacher *et al.* (eds), *Responses: Paul de Man's Wartime Journalism* (Lincoln: University of Nebraska Press, 1989), 404–25.

'Theater, Technics, Writing', *1–800*, (Fall 1989), 15–19.

'Upsetting the Setup: Remarks on Heidegger's Questing after Technics', *MLN*, 104 (1989), 976–91.

'The Vaulted Eye: Remarks on Knowledge and Professionalism', *Yale French Studies*, 77 (1990), 44–60.

'On the Balcony: The Theater of Technics', in L. Lambrechts and J. Nowe (eds), *Bild-Sprache: Texte zwischen Dichten und Denken* (Louvain: Louvain University Press, 1990), 283–97.

'Criticism Underway: Walter Benjamin's *Romantic Concept of Criticism*', in Kenneth R. Johnston *et al.* (eds), *Romantic Revolutions: Criticism and Theory* (Bloomington and Indianapolis: Indiana University Press, 1990), 302–19.

'Genealogy of Modernity: History, Myth and Allegory in Benjamin's *Origin of the German Mourning Play*', *MLN*, 106 (1991), 465–500.

'Deconstruction Before the Name', *Cardozo Law Review*, 13:4 (1991), 1181–90.

'The Media and the War', *Alphabet City* (Summer 1991), 22–26, reprinted in *Emergences*, 3–4 (1992), 16–26.

Return to Freud: Jacques Lacan's Dislocation of Psychoanalysis, rev. and expanded edn of German original, trans. Michael Levine (Cambridge: Cambridge University Press, 1991).

'In the Name of the Law', in Drucilla Cornell *et al.* (eds), *Deconstruction and the Possibility of Justice* (New York and London: Routledge, 1992), 232–57.

'Taking Exception to Decision: Walter Benjamin and Carl Schmitt', in Harry Kunneman and Hent de Vries (eds), *Enlightenments: Encounters between Critical Theory and Contemporary French Thought* (Kampen: Pharos, 1993), 141–61, also in *Diacritics*, 22:3–4 (1992), 5–18.

'Breaching the Gap: On Lacan's *Ethics of Psychoanalysis*', in Mark Poster (ed.), *Politics, Theory, and Contemporary Culture* (New York: Columbia University Press, 1993), 131–58.

'Objectivity Otherwise', in W. Natter *et al.* (eds), *Objectivity and its Other* (New York and London: Guilford Press, 1995), 33–50.

'Upping the Ante: Deconstruction as Parodic Practice', in Anselm Haverkamp (ed.), *Deconstruction Is/In America: A New Sense of the Political* (New York and London: New York University Press, 1995), 60–75.

'The Future of the University: The Cutting Edge', in Terry Smith (ed.), *Ideas of the University* (Sydney: Research Institute for the Humanities and Social Sciences, in association with Power Publications, 1996), 43–75.

Mass Mediauras: Form, Technics, Media (Stanford, CA: Stanford University Press, 1996).

'Reading – "to the end of the world"', *MLN*, 111 (1996), 819–34.

'Double Take: Acting and Writing in Genet's "L'étrange mot d' ..."', *Yale French Studies*, 91 (1997), 28–48.

Violence, Identity, and Self-Determination, ed. Hent de Vries and Samuel Weber (Stanford, CA: Stanford University Press, 1997).

'Benjamin's Writing Style', in *Encyclopedia of Aesthetics*, Vol. 1, ed. Michael Kelly (New York and Oxford: Oxford University Press, 1998), 261–64.

'Nomos in *The Magic Flute*', *Angelaki*, 3:2 (1998), 61–68.

'Family Scenes: Some Preliminary Remarks on Domesticity and Theatricality', *South Atlantic Quarterly*, 98:3 (1999), 22–28.

The Legend of Freud, expanded edn (Stanford, CA: Stanford University Press, 2000).

'Benjamin's Excitable Gestures', *Hybridity*, 1:1 (2000), 55–76.

'The Virtuality of Medium', *Sites*, 4:2 (2000), 297–319.

'Psychoanalysis and Theatricality', *Parallax*, 6:3 (2000), 29–48.

Religion and Media, eds. Hent de Vries and Samuel Weber (Stanford, CA: Stanford University Press, 2001).

Institution and Interpretation, expanded ed. (Stanford, CA: Stanford University Press, 2001).

'Replacing the Body: An Approach to the Question of Digital Democracy', in Marcel Henaff and Tracy Strong (eds), *Public Space and Democracy* (Minneapolis and London: University of Minnesota Press, 2001), 172–88.

Index